101 Preschool Reading Activities

Ages 3-6

By
Marsha Elyn Wright

Published by Totline® Publications
an imprint of

Published by Totline® Publications
An imprint of McGraw-Hill Children's Publishing

Send all inquiries to:
McGraw-Hill Children's Publishing
3195 Wilson Drive NW
Grand Rapids, Michigan 49544

101 Preschool Reading Activities—ages 3–6
ISBN: 1-57029-489-5

1 2 3 4 5 6 7 8 9 MAL 09 08 07 06 05 04

The McGraw-Hill Companies

Give Us a Hand

What better way to help children learn their own names and the names of their classmates than with personalized handprints! Title a bulletin board "Give Us a Hand!" Cover the board with yellow (or other bright color) butcher paper. Cut tagboard into 8" x 10" pieces, one for each child. Clearly write each child's name in large dashed-line letters at the bottom of each piece. Set out shallow pans of paint. Help each child place a hand into the paint and then both hands carefully on their tagboard piece above their printed name. Let dry. Laminate the pieces. Invite children to trace their names in crayon. Post the personalized handprints on the board. Encourage children to take turns pointing to their name and saying each letter aloud for the class.

NEWS Letter!

Prepare an alphabet display at children's eye level for your students to read as they go in and out the door! Cover the inside of your door with butcher paper. Add the title "NEWS Letter!" Give each child a page from a newspaper. Invite children to search for examples of a specific letter that you want to highlight for the week. Direct each child to circle the examples with crayon, cut them out, and glue them on the butcher paper. Encourage children to cut out as many examples as they can during the week and add them to the door. Challenge children to cover the door completely by the week's end.

Wall of Words

Help children understand that print carries messages and has meaning. Designate one area of your classroom as the "Wall of Words." Set out a box of old magazines and newspapers. Encourage children to search through for words they can "read" or ones they want to learn. After a child cuts out a word, encourage the child to come to you to help learn the word. Once children learn their words, invite them to tape their words on the wall. Each day, let children who found words point to them and read them aloud for the class!

Label It!

Display simple labels, signs, and printed directions in places that count. Meaningful labels build vocabulary and build beginning sight-reading skills. Define classroom activities by printing each label on a mini-sentence strip. Label your monitor, computer, printer, and other items of technology. Change labels as different puzzles, games, and materials are added to your classroom. Invite children to create the names. Set up a Writing Room, a Blocks Box, an Art Gallery, and a Playhouse. Supply a variety of materials and props, always setting out paper and pencils, and then encourage children to label their drawings and to create lists for their activities. As children move from one area to another, point out the labels. Children will soon learn that labels are words and that words tell us what things are. Before long children will be reading labels, too!

The Reading Room

Set up a comfy "Reading Room." Buy fabric remnants and pin up simple curtains on one wall above a cozy couch or pile of pillows. Add a rug to make this room inviting. Display a variety of books and magazines on a bookshelf. On one shelf, set out cassette players, headphones, and tapes to encourage children to listen to stories. Remind children to be quiet and courteous. To manage the flow of children in and out of your Reading Room, make a nametag for each child on a strip of sturdy paper. Pin up the tags in a line along the bottom of your board. Tell children that when they go to the Reading Room, they remove their nametags and use them as bookmarks. When they exit the Reading Room, have them pin up their bookmarks once again. You can easily see how many bodies are reading!

I Am Special

This activity will help children understand that words can describe thoughts and feelings. First, read aloud a book about positive self-concept, such as *The Mixed-Up Chameleon* by Eric Carle (HarperCollins, 1984) or *I Like Me!* by Nancy Carlson (Viking Penguin, 1988). Next, reproduce the *I Like Me!* picture frame and *I Am Special* thought bubble on pages 8-9 for each child. In front of a mirror, ask each child why they are special. Record the responses on the thought bubbles. Photograph each child and mount the print on one of the picture frames, or invite children to draw self-portraits. Mount the portraits on a bulletin board accompanied by their thought bubbles. Invite children to take turns "reading" their thoughts to the class. Periodically, encourage children to rewrite why they are special, and then share their new ideas with the class.

I Like Me!

Name

I Am Special

My name is

_______________________.

I am special. I can

7 It's Raining Words!

Decorate your classroom so it's raining words! Cut out large, wide raindrop shapes from blue paper. Punch a hole in each one and tie on a length of yarn, ribbon, or string. Cut out 26 puffy clouds from sturdy white paper. Print a different letter of the alphabet on each cloud. Hang the clouds from the ceiling. When children learn a new word, print it on a raindrop and attach it to the cloud displaying the beginning letter of the word. At the end of each day, ask for a volunteer to choose a cloud, say its letter, and read the raindrop words under the cloud.

8 Reader of the Day!

Let children use feathers, pompons, streamers, fabric scraps, and glittery materials to help decorate and label a Reader Chair. Reproduce the "Reader of the Day!" badge and bookmark on page 11, one for each child. Select a different child each Friday to be "Reader of the Day." At the beginning of the week, invite that child to color a reader badge and bookmark and to select a book to read to the class. Send the book home with a parent note, requesting that the family read the book each day with the child and return it on Friday. Make this a very special event. Invite parents to attend. Pin the badge on the reader. Place the Reader Chair in a prominent place. Encourage children to applaud the reader as he sits in the special chair and then to applaud again after the book is shared. Display the featured books so other children will be encouraged to read them!

Reader of the Day!

Post Office

Set up a Post Office. Collect and clean half-gallon milk cartons, one for each child. Cut off the top of each one, lay it on its side, and cover it with paper to make it a mailbox. You can also decorate small boxes, cutting a slit in each box. Print each child's name on a mailbox. Glue the boxes together in rows using alphabetical order by first names. Each week announce "Special delivery!" At that time, help each child print a word on an index card that they have learned. Collect the cards and select a Post Master who will mix them up and deliver one card inside each mailbox. At the end of the day, let children take turns trying to read their new special delivery word! Encourage children to take their words home to read to their families. Invite children to post friendly notes to their classmates in the mailboxes. What a great way to build an excitement for reading!

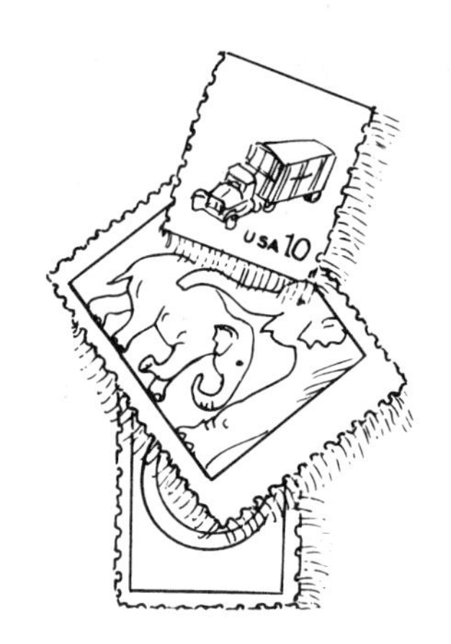

Read and Paint

Set up an easel, paint, and brushes outside. Have on hand newsprint on which to paint pictures. Print a very primary word that might inspire a picture, such as *heart, sun, happy, or house,* on an index card and display it on the easel. Let children take turns reading the word and painting a picture of it. Help children paint the word on their pictures. Display the artwork in a hallway or on a wall outside for other children to enjoy.

11 Rhyming Word Picture Cards

Reproduce the "Rhyming Word Picture Cards" on pages 14 and 15. Color the pictures and laminate them before cutting apart the cards. Separate the cards into two piles—one set of pictures in one pile and the matching rhyming cards in another pile. Have children sit in front of the board. Display one set of picture cards in the tray along the bottom of the board. Select a Leader to choose a card from the other pile and name the picture on it. Challenge children to find the rhyming picture word card on display. Direct children to raise their hands or stand up if they know the matching card. Let the Leader call on different children to pick out the rhyming card. If the card is a match, the child who identified it gets to be the new leader!

12 Super Words

Sit children in a circle. Write simple words that have rhyming words on separate index cards, one for each child. (Examples: cat, bed, pig, mop, tub, day, seat, ice, cone, cube) Read aloud each word one by one, challenging children to say a rhyming word. If a child thinks of a word, have that child stand up. If the rhyming word is correct, print it on the back of the matching word card and give it to the child. Do this for each word. Tell children these are their very own "Super Words." Reward children who can read both words at the end of the day!

Rhyming Word Picture Cards

cat

man

car

boy

bee

bun

wig

frog

hen

Rhyming Word Picture Cards

hat

pan

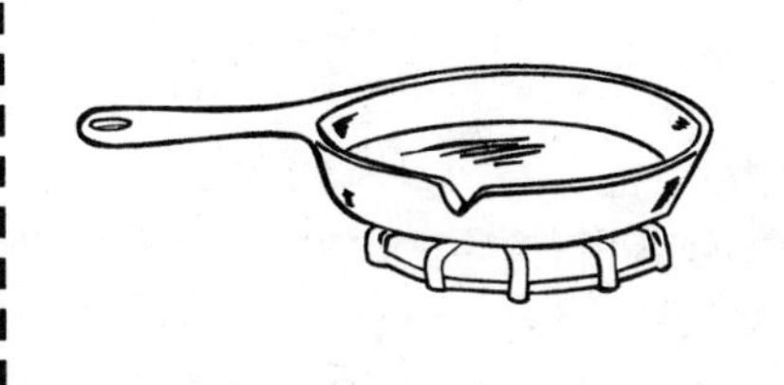

jar

toy

tree

sun

pig

dog

pen

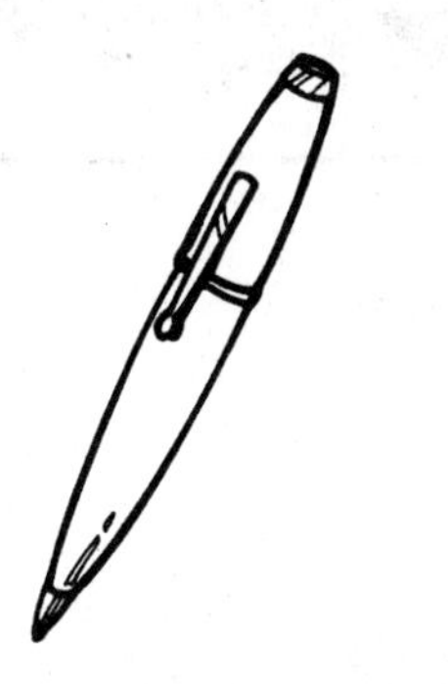

13 Farmer, Farmer

Invite children to name some of their favorite farm animals as they recite this open-ended rhyme. Print the rhyme with the blank lines on chart paper. Use a pointer to track the words as children recite the rhyme. Call on different children to name a favorite farm animal for each blank. (Use the plural form of the animal's name in the poem.) Afterwards, post the rhyme on a bulletin board. Direct children to draw a picture of their favorite farm animal. Help children write the names of their animals below their artwork. Post the hand-drawn animals around the rhyme.

"Farmer, Farmer"

Farmer, farmer, out in the sun,
I see your _____,
May I pet one?

Farmer, farmer, dressed all in blue,
I see your _____,
May I pet two?

Farmer, farmer, resting on your knee,
I see your _____,
May I pet three?

Farmer, farmer, please don't snore!
I see your _____,
May I pet four?

Farmer, farmer, by a beehive,
I see your _____,
May I pet five?

—Marsha Elyn Wright

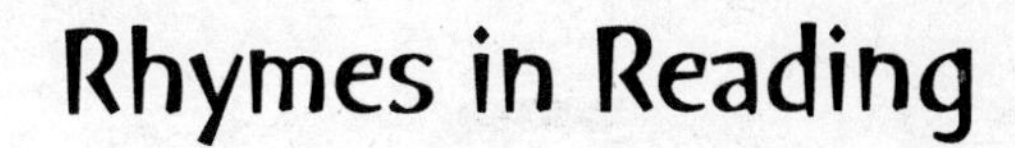

The Animal Parade

Copy "The Animal Parade" on chart paper. Ignite children's imaginations as you make up pairs of rhyming words from animal names to nonsense words, that complete the lines. When children say the name of an animal, encourage them to act or sound like the animal.

"The Animal Parade"

Marching, marching, 1, 2, 3!
Marching, marching, look and see,
Animals big and animals small,
Animals short and animals tall!

Examples:

Left, right, goes a little _____, dog
Marching beside a little, tiny _____. frog

Left, right, goes a giant _____, rhino
Marching beside a giant, big _____. dino

Left, right, goes a fuzzy _____, bat
Marching beside a fuzzy, furry _____. cat

Left, right, goes a funny _____, monkey
Marching beside a funny, silly _____. zunkey

(Repeat the first verse again to end the rhyme.)

–Marsha Elyn Wright

My Rhyming Book

Reproduce "My Rhyming Book" on pages 18-20 for each child. Let children dictate words for you to record that complete the sentences. Invite children to draw a picture that illustrates the word on each page. Have children draw a self-portrait on the last page of their books. Encourage children to read their books to their families. The pages are easily glued back to back and stapled in the middle.

I am a reader.
Listen to me!

My Picture

My Rhyming Book

Name

I can read

It rhymes with

1-57029-489-5 *101 Preschool Reading Activities*

It rhymes with

I can read

I Can Read That!

Cover the back of a bookcase with felt or flannel, tacking the edges into place. Think of a simple sentence frame and write each word on a separate card. (Example: A ____ is on the ____.) Attach Velcro® fasteners to the back of each word card. Pass out two flannelboard figures to each child. (See patterns on pages 26–28.) Arrange the word cards to form the sentence, leaving a large space for each blank. Let children take turns placing their figures within the blanks and reading the sentence.

What an Apron!

Make a flannelboard out of a two-pocket apron (available at most kitchen, import, or thrift stores). Sew a piece of felt on the apron above each pocket. Sew a different color to the front of each pocket. Don the apron, and you become a fun, unique flannelboard! Reproduce the *Rhyming Word Picture Cards* on pages 14–15. Attach a Velcro® fastener to the back of each card. Put one set of cards in one pocket and the matching set in the other pocket. Pull out a card from one pocket and display it on your flannelboard apron. Ask children to read the word. Pull out each card from the other pocket, one by one, and have children decide if it is the rhyming match for the first word. Once found, display the rhyming pair on your pockets and walk around the class, pointing to different children to read the words.

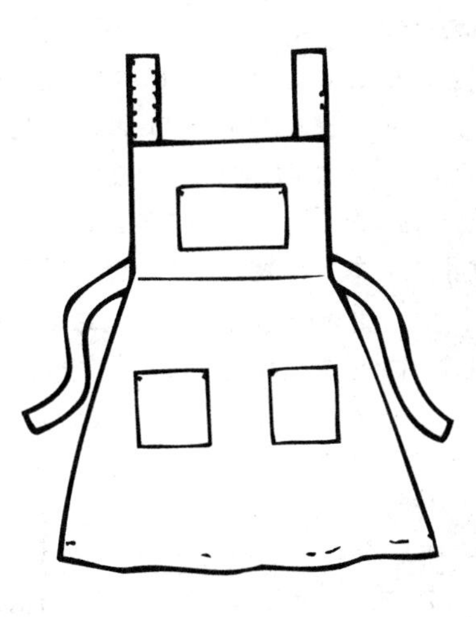

Flannelboards to Teach Reading

18 Flannelboard Sentences

Reproduce *Flannelboard Patterns*—A (page 26) on paper for each child. Invite children to color and cut out the animal shapes. Print this sentence frame on a sentence strip:

The ___ is ___.
(Leave lots of space for the blanks.)

Print the name of each animal on a separate word card. Make blank word cards by cutting up sentence strips. Attach Velcro® fasteners to the back of the sentence strip and each word card. Place the sentence frame on a flannelboard. Let children take turns taping one of their paper animals to the flannelboard. Display the word card that matches the animal within the sentence frame. Invite children to say words that could complete the sentence. Examples: The fish is blue. The fish is wiggly. The fish is wet. The fish is cute. Write each word on a blank card and place it on the flannelboard within the sentence. Encourage children to read the new sentence frame each time.

19 Flannelboard Opposites

Have fun teaching word opposites using a flannelboard! Print word opposites (in/out, over/under, and so on) on separate cards cut from tagboard. (Or, make copies of pages 56–58 on cardstock.) Attach Velcro® fasteners to the back of each card. Place a large felt square on your flannelboard. Give each child a flannelboard figure. (See pages 26–28 for patterns. Or, cut simple shapes from felt—heart, triangle, circle, moon, and so on.) Give a directive, such as "Put your shape over the square." "Put the matching word card (over) on the flannelboard." Ask a volunteer to follow your directions by positioning their figure in relation to the square. Give a new directive using the word opposite: "Put your shape under the square." Display the corresponding word card (under). Have the volunteer reposition their figure on the flannelboard. Repeat this several times so each child has an opportunity to manipulate a figure on the flannelboard.

20 Flannelboard Fun

Give each child a flannelboard figure. (See pages 26–28 for patterns.) Have children sit in a semi-circle. Display a large piece of felt or flannel on your white board. Describe one of the flannelboard figures by saying, I'm thinking of something that is ____. Challenge children to identify the figure. Invite the child holding the figure to place it on the flannelboard. After five figures are on the flannelboard, have children close their eyes while you remove one of the figures. When children open their eyes, invite them to try to guess which figure is missing. This activity not only builds vocabulary but also develops memory skills.

21 Oh, What a Feeling!

Use a flannelboard to teach children feeling words. Brainstorm with children words that describe how they feel, such as happy, sad, angry, and scared. Print each word on a tagboard strip and attach a "hooks" piece of Velcro® fastener to the back. Help children become familiar with the words. Copy this rhyme on chart paper. Place a large heart shape cut from felt on a flannelboard. Let children recite the rhyme with you. When you reach the end, place a feeling word on the heart. Have children read the word and express the emotion with their faces. Add excitement by taking a group picture of each emotion expressed. Display the photographs with their feeling cards on a bulletin board titled

"Oh, What a Feeling!"
I have a little feeling,
Deep inside of me,
It shows upon my face,
So everyone can see.
I feel ________.

—Marsha Elyn Wright

Flannelboards to Teach Reading

Animal Names

Make a set of felt flannelboard figures using the patterns on pages 26–28. Write the name of each figure on a tagboard strip and attach a "hooks" piece of a hook and loop fastener to the back. Pair up three animal names and three figures on a flannelboard. Have children read aloud the names with you. While children close their eyes, mix up the name cards and figures. When children open their eyes, challenge a volunteer to match the names and figures and read each name aloud. Repeat this several times using different figures and word cards.

Flannelboard Stories

Place some flannelboard figures in a paper sack. Display a flannelboard and have children sit around it in a semi-circle. Ask for a volunteer to remove two to four figures from the sack and name each one. Encourage the child to tell an imaginative story about the figures as they manipulate them on the flannelboard. Repeat this several times.

Pretend Painting

Attach a large piece of felt or flannel to an easel. Place a set of flannelboard alphabet letters and paintbrushes near the flannelboard. Invite children to spell their names on the flannelboard and then to use the paintbrushes to paint over each letter. Add to the fun by having children wear their painting smocks as they pretend to paint!

Flannelboards to Teach Reading

25 Flannelboard Spelling

Collect small squares of flat indoor-outdoor carpeting (one for each child) to use as individual flannelboards. Buy multiple sets of felt alphabet letters. Print simple sight words (and, boy, girl, the, cat . . .) on separate cards, one or two for each child. Give each child a word card. Spread out the alphabet letters. Let children find the alphabet letters that spell their words and arrange them on their carpet sqares. When children have spelled a word correctly, have them return the alphabet letters to the floor. Have them choose a new word card and try to spell it. Give children plenty of time for this activity so they each spell as least four words on their flannelboard.

26 Round-Robin Stories

Giving children practice in oral language can be loads of fun. Spread out your flannelboard figures. Display a flannelboard. Invite children to make up a round-robin story. You need to begin a simple story using two or three figures on the flannelboard. Model for children how to first describe each character you are placing in the story. (Example: Once upon a time there was a flat-footed, fuzzy yellow duck with a bad cold. He'd cough and sneeze, "ACHHOOO!" Along came his friend, a black-spotted dog with big ears. . . .) Ask for volunteers to take turns choosing a figure, describing it, and then manipulating it on the flannelboard to continue the story. After all the figures have been used, finish the story for your class. These stories usually turn out silly, invoking lots of laughter from children and even you!

Flannel Board Patterns – A

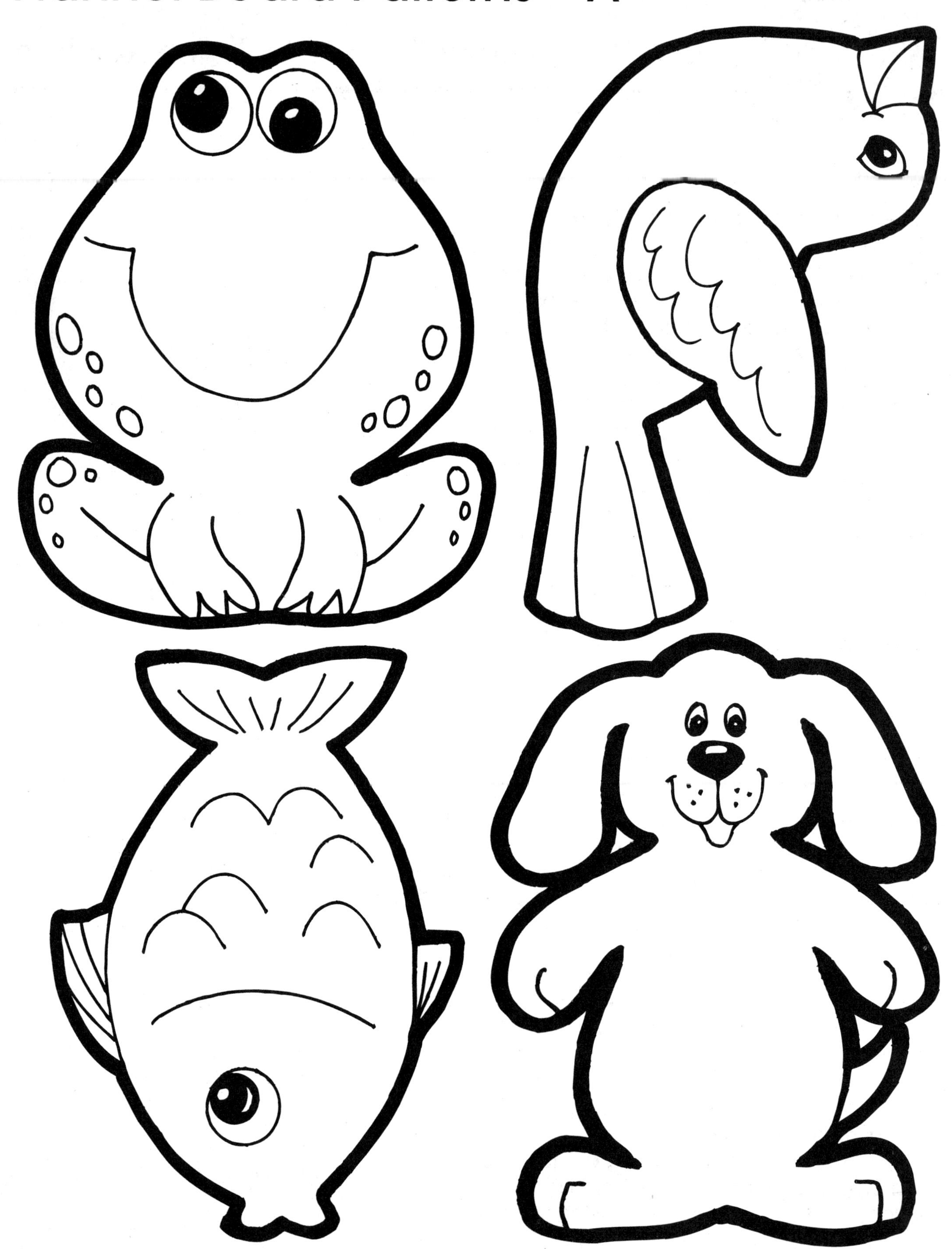

Flannel Board Patterns – B

Flannel Board Patterns – C

Interviews

As children engage in independent play, walk around the classroom with a pretend microphone, giving "people-on-the-street" interviews about what children are doing. Invite each child to invent a story about their activity. Write everything down exactly as the child dictates the story to you. During classroom story time, read aloud the stories and applaud the authors. Show children that reading is interesting by your enthusiasm. Let children illustrate their stories and take them home to share with their families.

Story Time Skits

Most young children love to be theatrical! Choose a simple folk tale to retell, such as "The Little Red Hen" or "Goldilocks and the Three Bears." Set up simple props and collect a variety of hats, one for each character. Ask for volunteers to wear the hats and act out the story as you tell it. Invite the audience to take an active role in the storytelling. Make simple signs that say Ooh! and Ahh! Encourage the audience to call out "ooh" and "ahh" as you hold up each sign during various parts of the story. By involving children in the reading activity, you will motivate them to work towards learning to read.

Mystery Reader

Send home a letter inviting parents to sign up to be a "Mystery Reader" in your classroom. You might provide parents with a list of appropriate book titles that are available in the school library that they can check out to retell or read to your class. Tell parents that their appointed date is to be kept a secret so children do not know who will be reading to them. Decorate a chair especially for the Mystery Reader. Before the event, play a guessing game with children by inviting them to ask yes and no questions that help them identify the Mystery Reader. List children's guesses and print their name by their guess. Photograph children with the Mystery Reader and post it on a bulletin board. Spend time asking open-ended questions about the story so children may build their language skills and better understand that reading is a way to communicate ideas and obtain information. Let children help you write and illustrate a group thank-you letter.

Listen and Move!

Let children work out their wiggles and play an active role in your storytelling. Whenever you are reading a story and a character starts to march, walk, run, or sing, stop reading and have children pretend to be that character and mimic its movements. Direct children to sit down as you continue the story until the next action. If characters call out or shout a word or phrase repeatedly, prompt children to do the same. This is a fun way to focus children's attention on how important it is to listen carefully.

Read It Again!

Here is a suggested list of book titles that are fun to read aloud to young children:

Bear Noel by Olivier Dunrea (Farrar, Straus, and Giroux, 2000): Animals of the north woods are thrilled when they hear Bear Noel coming.

The Happy Hedgehog Band by Martin Waddell (Candlewick Press, 1992): Hedgehogs invite their animal friends to accompany their band with lots of lively sounds.

Harry the Dirty Dog by Gene Zion (Harper & Row, 1965): Harry does everything he possibly can to avoid a bath!

The Mixed-Up Chameleon by Eric Carle (HarperCollins, 1984): A bored chameleon wishes it were like zoo animals.

Mouse's Birthday by Jane Yolen (G.P. Putnam, 1993): Mouse's house grows smaller as his friends squeeze in.

Mouse Count by Ellen Stoll Walsh (Harcourt Brace Jovanovich, 1991): Ten mice outwit a sneaky snake!

Not Yet, Yvette by Helen Ketteman (Albert Whitman, 1992): A girl and her father plan a surprise party.

Walking Through the Jungle by Julie Lacome (Candlewick Press, 1993): A marching boy imagines jungle creatures.

When the Goblins Came Knocking by Anna Grossnickle Hines (Greenwillow, 1995): This Halloween is different!

Wolf Plays Alone by Dominic Catalano (Philomel, 1992): A wolf is joined by a lively group of animal musicians.

The Wonderful Feast by Esphyr Slobodkina (Greenwillow, 1993): A horse's leftovers is a feast for other farm animals.

Story Time

Read to children frequently, establishing regular reading times throughout the day. Choose a story with two or three main characters, such as *How Joe the Bear and Sam the Mouse Got Together* by Beatrice Schenk de Regniers (Lothrop, Lee and Shepherd Books, 1990). Model for children how a fluent reader sounds by reading expressively and effortlessly. Pick out a repetitious phrase that each character says in the story. Practice changing your voice as you say the phrases. For example, use a high-pitched, squeaky voice for Sam the mouse and a deep, low voice for Joe the bear.

Assign small groups of children the different movements or gestures that the different characters perform. You might bring bells to ring, sticks to hit, or sand blocks to scrape, and assign each group a sound effect. Nothing gets children's attention more than being involved!

As you read, explain words children might not know. Point out how each illustration relates to the story. Encourage children to talk about the characters' feelings and behaviors. Look for ways to relate what is happening in the story to activities children might be experiencing.

Encourage children to comment on the story and describe their favorite parts. Invite individuals to retell the story in their own words. By doing these activities, you will help children better understand the relationship between printed letters and words, and sound and print.

33 Days of the Week

Invite children to practice learning the days of the week in order by singing the following song:

"Just Now"
(Sing to the tune of "Clementine"
or "Found a Peanut")
Sunday, Monday, Tuesday, Wednesday,
Thursday, Friday, Saturday,
Just now we named the week days,
Named the week days, just now!

34 You Are My Sunshine

Everyone loves singing "You Are My Sunshine!" Make it an action song with this activity. Reproduce the song props on page 34, one set for each child and four extra copies for you. Color and cut out four yellow suns, one happy face, one gray cloud, and one red heart. Write the song title and chorus on chart paper. As you are writing, whenever you come to these key words—sunshine, happy, gray, and love—paste the paper props in their place. Teach children the tune and words to the song. Invite them to color and cut out their props. Guide them in reading each of the prop words. Help children glue each prop onto a craft stick. Then sing! As children read and sing the song, prompt them to hold up the corresponding prop for each line.

Demonstrate how to make an envelope in which to store the props. Help each child fold an 8 1/2" x 11" sheet of construction paper in half "like a hamburger bun" and staple two sides. (Do not staple the edges opposite the fold closed.)

"You Are My Sunshine"

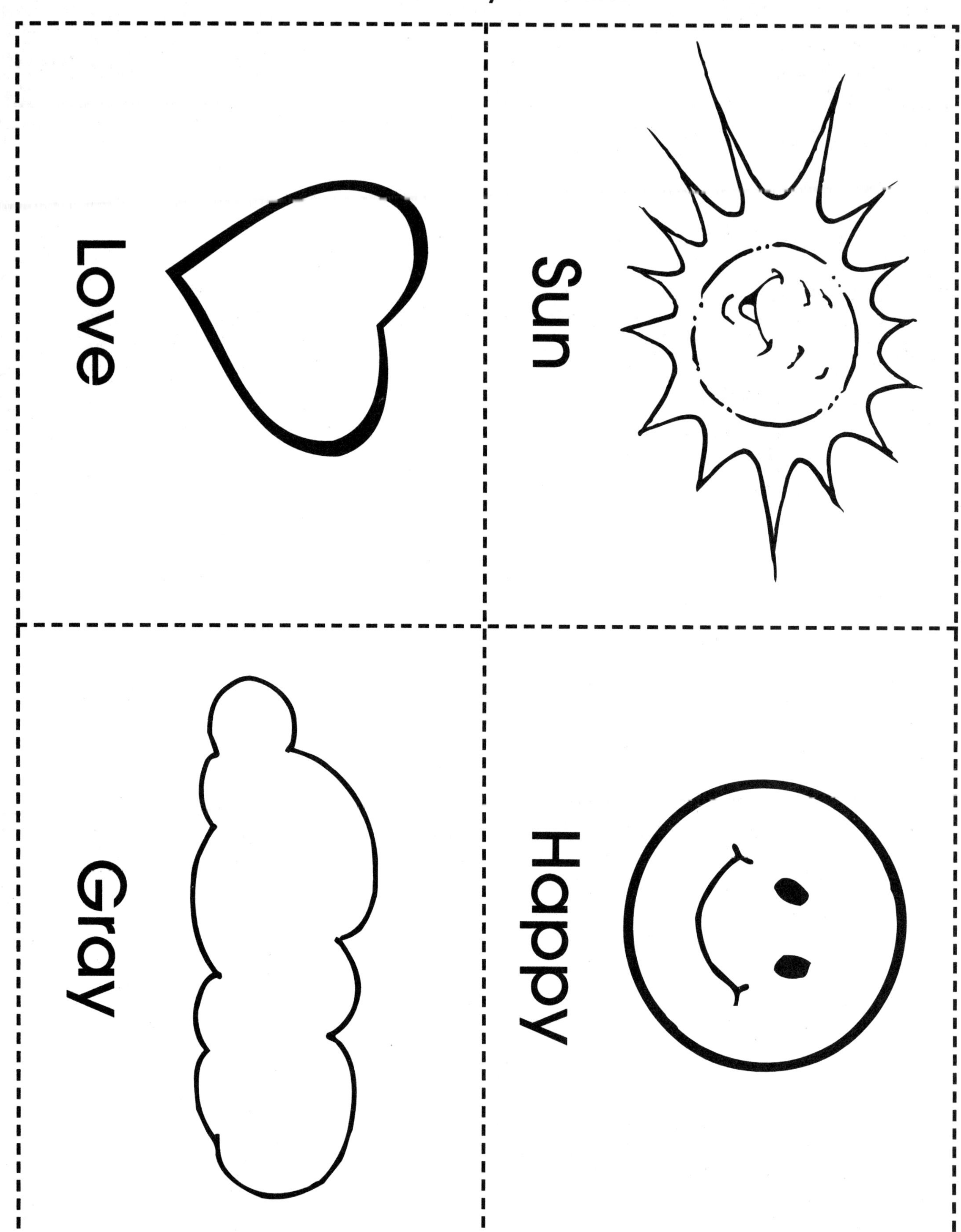

1-57029-489-5 *101 Preschool Reading Activities*

35 Reading in Tune

Invite children to play "Reading in Tune." Arrange chairs in a large circle, placing a book under each chair. Play lively music. Invite children to march around the inside of the circle in time to the music. When you stop the music, direct each child to sit on the nearest chair and begin "reading" the book that is underneath it. When the music starts again, prompt children to return their books under their chairs and pick up the march once again. Repeat this several times. After playing, display the books in a corner titled "Reading in Tune" so children can finish reading the books that caught their imaginations.

36 I'd Like to Meet

An important goal for young children is to learn their names and those of their classmates. Help them achieve this through song! Print each child's name on a strip of tagboard, punch holes in each strip, and tie on yarn. Have children wear their nametags when you teach them new words to a traditional favorite—"Apples and Bananas."

"I'd Like to Meet"

I'd like to meet, meet, meet,
Smatty, latty, Patty,
I'd like to meet, meet, meet,
Hilly, dilly, Billy!

I'd like to meet, meet, meet,
Win, wan, Juan.
I'd like to meet, meet, meet . . .
(Make up nonsense rhyming words for each child's name, and then sing your own name in song!)

Sing-Along Books

There are many exciting picture books to "sing read" to children. Here are just a few!

A-Hunting We Will Go! by Steven Kellogg (Morrow Junior Books, 1998): A modern version of this children's song presents a lively telling!

The Completed Hickory Dickory Dock by Jim Aylesworth (Atheneum, 1990): This describes what happened after the mouse ran up the clock.

Inch by Inch: The Garden Song by David Mallett (HarperCollins, 1997): Child grows a garden in song!

The Marvelous Toy by Tom Paxton (William Morrow, 1996): A father gives his son a fantastic toy.

Old MacDonald Had a Farm illustrated by Carol Jones (Houghton Mifflin, 1989): A cutaway peephole challenges the reader to guess which animal comes next.

This Old Man illustrated by Carol Jones (Houghton Mifflin, 1990): Readers look through a peephole to guess the next object the Old Man plays.

The Wheels on the Bus illustrated by Sylvie Kantorovitz Wickstrom (Crown, 1988): This traditional favorite is delightfully illustrated and is one in a series called "Raffi Songs to Read©."

38 It's Time for a Story

Reproduce the signs (page 38) on tagboard, color it, and laminate it for durability. Invite different children to hang up the sign on your classroom doorknob to avoid interruptions during story time. Call children to the rug for storytelling by choosing a movement that relates to one of the characters in the story. For example, direct children to soar silently like a hawk or hop quickly like a frog to the story rug. This movement helps get rid of the wiggles and builds excitement for storytelling!

39 Story Telling Methods

There are four basic types of storytelling that are appropriate for young children:

- Tell a story exactly as the author intended, pausing to show each illustration.
- Tell a story in your own words as you display each illustration.
- Tell a story using props.
- Tell a story by dramatizing it with movement.

Each way keeps children focused and interested. Choose stories that have repetitious words so children can join in the story when it is appropriate. Choose stories that have characters in action so children can mimic those actions. Give each child a bell to ring when it is time to turn a page.

Have volunteers stand up and act like one of the characters as you pause during your storytelling. The more involved children are in the telling of the story, the more they will pay attention and the more they will learn!

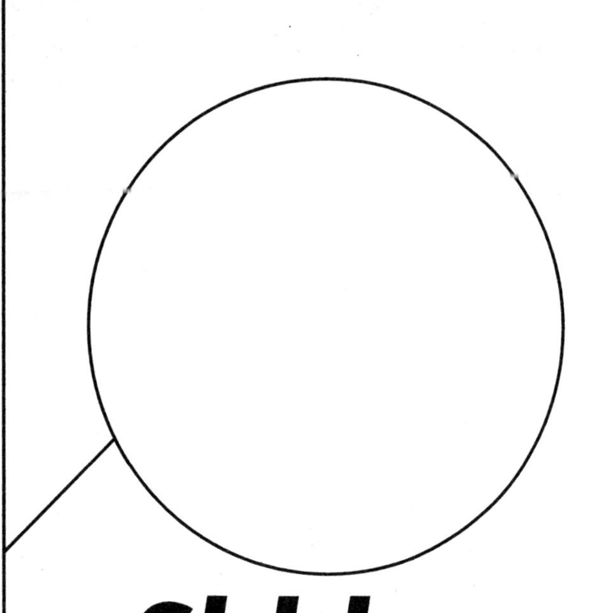

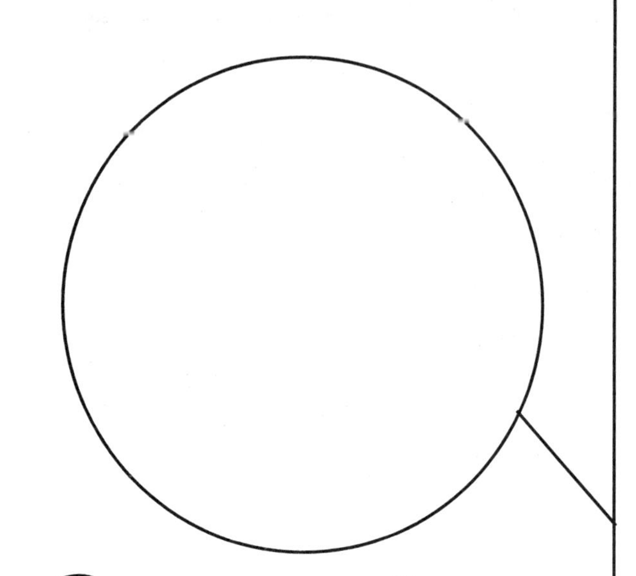

Shhh...

it's reading time!

Come In...

we're learning

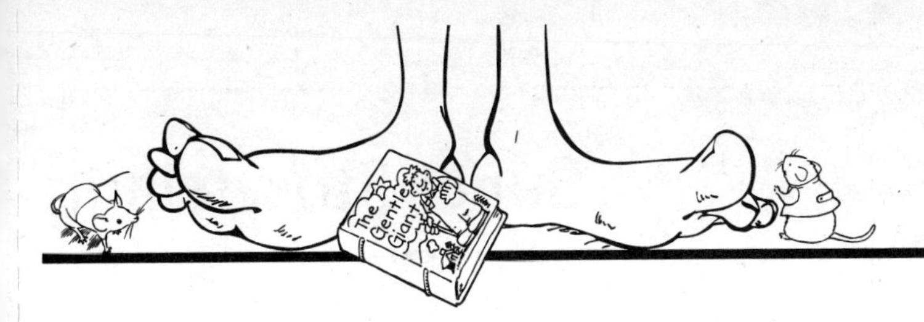

Roll a Story!

Empty a small, cube-shaped box, such as a tissue box. Reproduce the pictures below, cut them out, and glue each one on a side of the box to make a story cube. Start a simple story. (Example: Once upon a time there were two friends.) Invite a child to roll the story cube. When the cube lands, weave the object or animal displayed on top into your story. Invite another child to roll the cube and continue the tale. Let children take turns rolling the cube until the story is done. By helping to create the story, children will surely be attentive during story time!

Star Storytellers

Set up a "Star Storyteller for the Day" in your classroom. Cut out magazine pictures that tell a story, and mount each one at the top of a large sheet of construction paper, one for each child. Let each child select a picture, think about what is happening in it, and make up a story about it. Ask parent volunteers to help you record children's stories exactly as they dictate them. Write each child's words below his picture and on the back of the paper, if necessary. Reproduce the "Star Storyteller Crown" on page 41 on sturdy paper, one for each child. Attach strips of construction paper to each side so it fits a child's head. Select a Star Storyteller, and have them decorate a crown using sequins, feathers, markers, and other sparkly materials. During a special story time, have the Star Storyteller hold up his picture as you enthusiastically read the story. Encourage children to applaud the storyteller as they walk to the front of the class after the storytelling is done. Take a photograph of each Star Storyteller holding up their story. Display these photos next to their corresponding stories on a bulletin board covered with cutout stars and titled "Star Storytellers."

Clay Characters

As you are storytelling, shape and reshape a llarge ball of clay into the different characters or objects in the story. Children will find it easier to focus on the storytelling as they watch your hands shape the characters. It will relax them and distractions will seem to disappear. You needn't worry about your own artistic talent. Children's imaginations will take over if your duck looks like a rock with legs!

Star Storyteller Crown

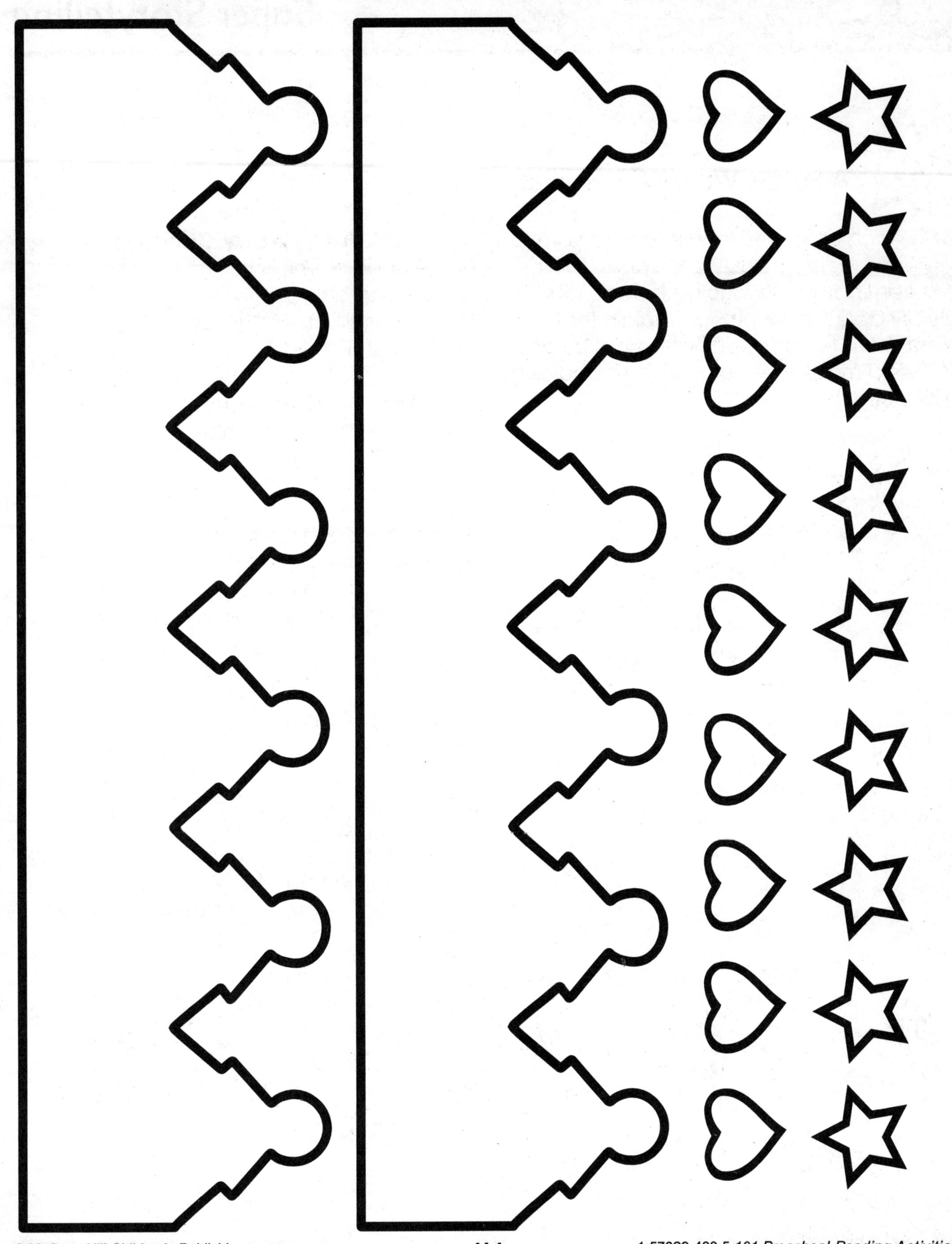

A Fuzzy, Wuzzy Caterpillar

Give each child a 12-inch length of yarn to represent a fuzzy, wuzzy caterpillar. Tell children that you are going to teach them a story about a caterpillar. Explain that you want them to hold their caterpillars by one end and move them around their bodies as you recite the story.

"A Fuzzy, Wuzzy Caterpllar"

Once upon a time,
Not so long ago,
Crawled a silly, fuzzy, wuzzy
Caterpillar named "Jo."

Jo moved along my arm,
Jo moved along my nose,
Jo moved along my head
And moved along my toes!

Jo moved along my knee,
Jo moved along my hips,
Jo moved along my feet
And moved along my lips!

Jo moved along my hand,
Jo moved along my eyes,
Jo moved along my back
And moved along my thighs!

Once upon a time,
Not so long ago,
Crawled a silly, fuzzy, wuzzy
Caterpillar named "Jo."

—Marsha Elyn Wright

1-57029-489-5 *101 Preschool Reading Activities*

Balloon Buddies

Imaginations will soar with this idea. Purchase helium-filled latex balloons, one for each child. Before school, tie a balloon to each child's chair. Invite children to think of a story about playing together with their new "balloon buddies." Direct children to illustrate their stories. Invite parent volunteers to walk around the room, letting each child dictate a story and recording the exact words near the artwork. Photograph each child with her art and balloon. Display the photos on a board titled "Balloon Buddies." Invite each child to hold her balloon as you read aloud the child's story. Let children take home their balloons and stories to share with their families.

Weather Stories

Reproduce the "Weather Symbol Patterns" on page 44, one for each child. Invite children to color the pictures and cut out the circles. Give each child a wide strip of paper. Demonstrate how to glue the patterns, in any order, side by side along the top of a strip. Point to each symbol and ask what kind of weather it represents. Talk about the activities children might do in each type of weather and the clothing they might wear. Invite each child to draw a self-portrait under each symbol, showing the clothes for that type of weather, and have them show an outdoor activity. Let children take turns telling their weather stories.

Weather Symbol Patterns

46 Tiny Tim

Print the poem "Tiny Tim" (page 46) on chart paper. Teach children the poem before inviting them to recite it. Act out the words with puppets! To make a quick puppet stage for each child, fold a paper plate in half and cut a slit from the center of the fold down to the ridged portion. Open the plate, and you'll find a slit across the center. Reproduce the poem and the turtle puppet (page 46) for each child. Have children color the turtle, cut it out, and glue it to one end of a large craft stick. Direct children to draw a bathtub on their puppet stages above the ridged portion.

Have children glue the poem box to the back of their plate. Model how to hold the stage with one hand and place the stick puppet in the slit with the other hand to move the turtle while reciting the poem.

47 Ollie Owl

Make each child a unique puppet stage out of a toilet paper tube. For each stage, cut a hole about the size of a fifty-cent piece in the front of the tube to make a tree trunk with a nesting hole. Tape real or paper branches to the top of the trunk. Reproduce the poem "Ollie Owl" and the owl puppet (page 47) for each child. Direct children to cut out the poem box and glue it to back of their tube. Have each child color the owl, cut it out, and glue it to one end of a large craft stick. Demonstrate how to use the stage by holding the tree with one hand and inserting a stick puppet through the bottom of the tube, having the owl peep into view through the hole.

Copy the poem on chart paper and teach children the words before letting them act out the poem with their owl puppets.

Tiny Tim Poem and Puppet

Tiny Tim

I have a tiny turtle.
His name is Tiny Tim.
I put him in the tub
To see him swim.
He drank all the water.
He ate all the soap.
Tiny, tiny bubbles,
Popped out of his throat!
Bubble! Bubble! Pop!

Ollie Owl Poem and Puppet

Ollie Owl

I have a fluffy friend
Who plays with me.
He's got big eyes
And lives in a tree.
He flies up and down
And peeks at me.
He flies all around
And hoots with glee.
Whooty! Whoo!
Whooty! Whoo!

—Marsha Elyn Wright

48 Spider Puppets

Teach children how to make simple finger puppets. First, roll and tape the ends together of a 2" x 3" strip of paper to make a tube. Slide it onto one of your fingers and decorate it to go with your story. Help each child make five spider finger puppets to act out the poems below. To make a spider puppet, cut slits along the bottom of the paper to make eight legs. Print "Five Little Spiders" and "The Itsy-Bitsy Spiders" (a twist on the traditional rhyme) on chart paper. Teach children the poems to become familiar with the words. Encourage them to recite each poem using their spider finger puppets.

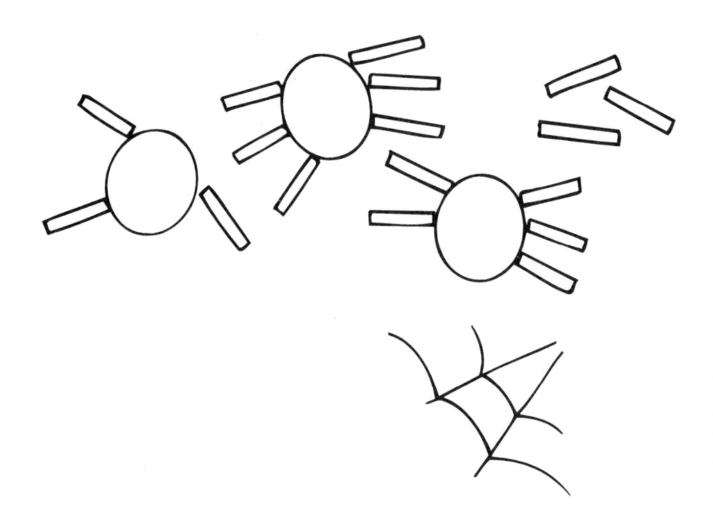

"Five Little Spiders"

Five little spiders sitting on a sink,
The first one said, "This is slippery, I think!"
The second one said, "I hear people in the room."
The third one said, "What's that Boom! Boom! Boom?"
The fourth one said, "Let's run and run and run!"
The fifth one said, "Let's go and have some fun!"
Then swish went the water and out went the light,
And the five little spiders crawled right out of sight!

—Marsha Elyn Wright

"The Itsy-Bitsy Spiders"

The itsy-bitsy spiders climbed up the garden hose,
Whoosh! went the water on a red, red rose,
Off jumped the spiders landing on a drain,
And the itsy-bitsy spiders climbed up the hose again!

—Marsha Elyn Wright

49 The Grumpy Troll

A simple puppet stage can be made out of a rectangular tissue box. For each stage, cut a second large hole in the bottom of the tissue box. After helping children make their stages, show them how to decorate the boxes with paper scraps, crepe paper streamers, fabric, and other materials. Reproduce the "Grumpy Troll Puppet Patterns" on page 50 for each child. Help children cut out the patterns, color them, and glue each one onto a craft stick. Print "The Grumpy Troll" on chart paper and teach children the poem. Demonstrate how to have a partner hold the decorated box while you insert the puppets from below through the holes to perform the poem on stage. Recite the poem together, letting children act it out using their puppets.

"The Grumpy Troll"

There was a grumpy troll
Who had a creaky knee.
He wanted to be friends
With a silly silly bee.

But when he said, "Hello,"
He growled, Grrrrr! instead,
And the silly silly bee
Went and bit his furry head!

There was a grumpy troll
Who had a funny wig.
He wanted to be friends
With a silly silly pig.

But when he said, "Hello,"
He growled, Grrrrr! instead,
And the silly silly pig
Went and bit his furry head!

So home went the troll
To mend his hurting head.
And the silly bee and pig
Brought him tea and jam and bread!

—Marsha Elyn Wright

Grumpy Troll Puppet Patterns

50 Circle Puppets

Add pizzazz to fingerplays with super-simple finger puppets. Purchase plain circle stickers in a variety of colors. Give children stickers to attach to the ends of their fingers. Show how to draw faces on the stickers for instant puppets! Encourage children to wear these puppets as they recite and perform the following fingerplays.

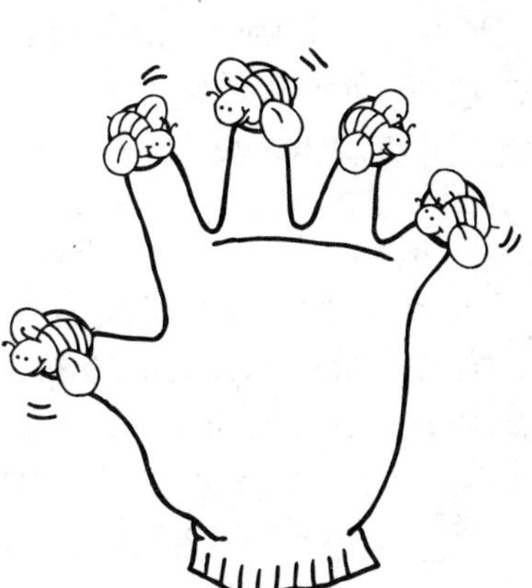

"Two Little Rabbits"

Two little rabbits hopping on a hill,
(Move each pointer finger up and down.)
One said, "I won't!"
(Move one finger back and forth.)
The other said, "I will!"
(Bend one finger up and down.)
One ate a carrot,
(Bend one finger as if "eating.")
The other ran away.
(Put one finger behind back.)
They hopped back together
(Move each pointer finger up and down.)
To play and play and play!
(Move fingers in any fun way.)

—Marsha Elyn Wright

"Here Is the Beehive"

Here is the beehive, but where are the bees?
(Fist with thumb hidden to make hivo.)
Hidden away so nobody sees.
(Place other hand over hive.)
Watch and you'll see them come out of the hive,
(Watch hive.)
One, two, three, four, five!
(Slowly straighten fingers one by one.)
Buzzzzz . . .
(Fingers "fly" away.)

51 Folded-Paper Finger Puppets

Try making folded-paper finger puppets to add excitement to fingerplays. For each puppet, cut a 5" x 5" square out of construction paper. Fold it in half lengthwise and then in half again to make a narrow strip. Position it so it looks like a tall rectangle. Roll the top end down to make a loop (the puppet's head) and attach a paper clip to hold it in place. Demonstrate how to draw a face on the puppet. Slip your finger into the folded section at the bottom of the puppet to finish. Help each child make at least one puppet. Encourage children to wear these puppets as they perform the following fingerplay.

"Five Little Bears"

Five little bears eating jam and bread,
(Move five fingers as if "eating.")
One got sick and went to bed.
(Bend one finger down.)
Papa Bear called Mama, and Mama said,
(Hold up two fingers from other hand.)
"No more bears eating jam and bread!"
(Move "Mama" finger back and forth.)
(Repeat with four bears, three bears, two bears, and then add the following verse.)

One little bear eating jam and bread,
(Move one finger as if "eating.")
He got sick and went to bed.
(Bend that finger down.)
Papa Bear called Mama, and Mama said,
(Hold up two fingers from other hand.)
"Now no more bears will eat jam and bread!"
(Move "Mama" finger back and forth.)

—Marsha Elyn Wright

52 Walking Puppets

Motivate children to perform fingerplays by demonstrating how to make puppets that walk! Cut out a simple body and head shape from cardstock, making two shapes for each child. Help children cut or punch out two finger-size holes at the bottom of their puppets. Model for children how to insert their middle and index fingers into the holes, moving their fingers to make the puppet walk. Encourage children to add hair, eyes, mouth, clothes, and other details to their puppets. Have children wear these walking puppets as they perform the following fingerplay.

"Mr. Right, Mrs. Left"

This is Mr. Right,
He stands up tall.
(Raise up puppet on right hand.)
This is Mrs. Left,
She's very, very small.
(Raise up puppet on left hand, then lower it.)
Say, "Hello," Mrs. Left.
(Wave puppet on left hand back and forth.)
Say, "Hello," Mr. Right.
(Wave puppet on right hand back and forth.)
Together they went walking
And kept talking through the night!
(Walk puppets together. Bend them up and down.)

—Marsha Elyn Wright

Five Tiny Pumpkins

Demonstrate how to make these simple finger puppets from heavy paper. For each puppet, cut out a rectangle about 2" x 3 1/2". Cut slits into the top of one end and at the bottom of the other end of the rectangle. Model for children how to join the ends around a finger by sliding one slit on top of the other slit. Encourage children to decorate their puppets to look like pumpkins for this fingerplay.

"Five Tiny Pumpkins"

Five tiny pumpkins sitting on a gate,
(Rest puppets on empty hand.)
One called out, "My it's getting late!"
(Wiggle one puppet.)
Two called out, "There's something in the air!"
(Wiggle two puppets.)
Three called out, "It's giving us a scare!"
(Wiggle three puppets.)
Four called out, "Let's run away and hide!"
(Wiggle four puppets.)
Five called out, "Let's quickly go inside!"
(Wiggle five puppets.)
So they all ran home and turned on the light,
(Make five puppets "run away.")
And huddled close together all Halloween night!
(Cover puppet hand with empty hand.)

—Marsha Elyn Wright

Find a Partner

Play "Find a Partner." Hold up each pair of opposite cards on pages 56–58 so children become familiar with the words. Tape one word on the back of each child without letting the child know the word. Challenge children to find their partners—those wearing the matching word opposites. Tell partners to stand back to back until everyone is paired up!

Reading Raceway

Play "Reading Raceway." Separate the opposite cards into two piles. Use one set to lay down a "racetrack" on a table at a center. Place the other pile nearby. Invite children, one at a time, to turn over a card from the pile and place it on top of its matching word opposite on the racetrack. Let children work in pairs to help each other "race" up and down the track to see how long it takes to match all the word opposites!

Word Detectives

Play "Word Detectives." Separate the opposite cards into two groups. Hide one group of cards around the room. Give each child one of the matching word opposites. Let children pretend to be Word Detectives searching for their matching word opposites. Remind children that if they find a word card that does not match their word, to leave it where it is for the right detective to find!

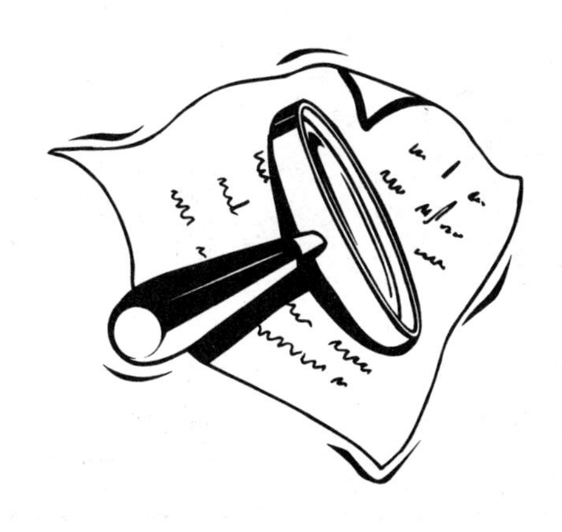

Opposite Cards–A

in

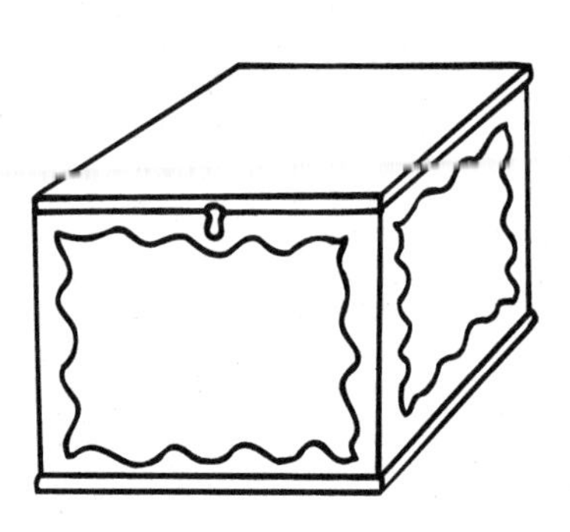

out

big

little

above

below

hot

cold

Opposite Cards–B

happy

sad

old

new

wet

dry

over

under

Opposite Cards–C

Colors

Teach children how to play "Colors." Collect eight different solid color circle stickers. Place each sticker on the left side of a separate index card. Print the name of the color on the right side of each card. Cut each index card in half in a different way (curved, zigzag, etc.) to make the resulting two-piece puzzle self-correcting. Place the color name halves on a table at a center. Put the sticker halves in a basket. Invite children to take turns finding the matching halves and putting together each puzzle.

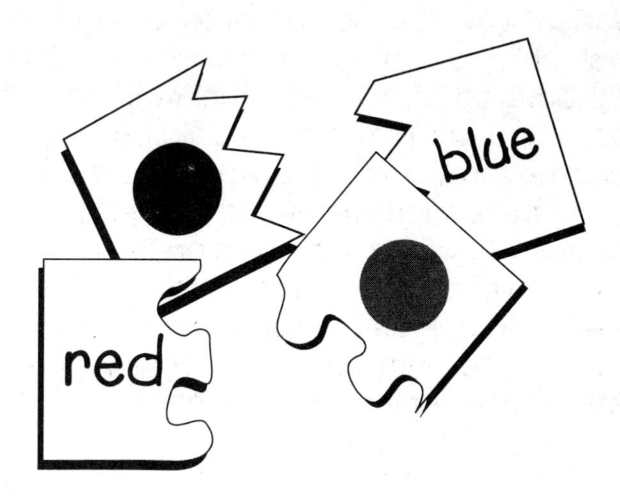

Guessing Game

Invite children to play "Guessing Game." Cut large circles from several colors of paper. Print the name of each color on the circle. Direct children to sit in a circle. Ask a child to help you lay the shapes in the circle so everyone can see them. Point to each shape and prompt children to "read" its color name. While children close their eyes, choose one child to hide a shape behind him. When the other children open their eyes, see who can be the first one to guess which color is hiding!

Follow the Leader

Teach children this version of "Follow the Leader." Lay down a carpet square for each child to sit upon. Print action words on tagboard cards, such as jump, run, march, hop, stand, and smile. Help children become familiar with the words. Hold up one of the action words and challenge children to act out the words on their squares without saying the word aloud. Listen to the giggles as someone emerges as the leader with everyone following the action, whether it's right or wrong!

One Day When I Went Walking

"One Day When I Went Walking" will help children learn number words as well as build memory skills. Print the number words one through ten on separate cards so you have one card for each child. (You will repeat numbers.) Pass out the cards and help children to read their number word. Put an animal toy for each child inside a bag. Invite children to sit in a circle and lay their number cards in front of them. Let one child draw a toy out of the bag and hold it up. Prompt the child to say, One day when I went walking, I saw (child's number word) (name of toy animal). For example, if a child who has the number three pulls out a toy elephant, she would say, "One day when I went walking, I saw three elephants." Pass the bag to the next child who pulls out a new animal. Have them repeat what the first child said as well as their own sentence. Laughter and fun will ensue as the bag is passed from child to child. Children will beg to play again and again, especially if you join in as the last storyteller!

Fill-in-the-Blank Mini-Books

Fill-in-the-blank mini-books are fun for young children to make and read. The story will be different every time you do one! Create simple, open-ended mini-books by stapling together four wide strips of paper for each eight-page book.

Page 1—I went to the farm.
Page 2—I saw a big _____.
Page 3—I saw a tiny _____.
Page 4—I saw a brown _____.
Page 5—I saw a black _____.
Page 6—I saw a funny _____.
Page 7—I saw a furry _____.
Page 8—I saw what I saw on the farm!

Page 1—I was VERY hungry.
Page 2—I ate a green _____.
Page 3—I ate a purple _____.
Page 4—I ate a red _____.
Page 5—I ate a yellow _____.
Page 6—I ate a blue _____.
Page 7—I ate an orange _____.
Page 8—I am VERY full!

Sticker Books

Assemble some blank eight-page mini-books. Choose a theme for each book and buy stickers that follow the theme—zoo animals, pets, farm animals, flowers, and so on. Place one theme-oriented sticker on every page of each book. Let children take turns selecting a book and "reading" it to the class. Prompt children to make up stories to go with the stickers.

Mini-Book Book Bag

Reproduce the three mini-books on pages 63-68. (Each book is designed to be photocopied on both sides of one sheet of paper.) Color and laminate the pages before assembling them into books. To assemble a book, cut the page in half along the solid line, fold on the dotted lines, arrange the mini-pages in order. Staple them together along the spine. Place the mini-books in a special cloth "Book Bag" along with objects that represent the stories, one item per story. Choose a different child each day to select the day's story and its object from your Book Bag. After a child selects a book, invite the child to write her name on the bag with a fabric pen.

Let children take turns bringing the Book Bag home. Attach a short note that invites parents to sign their names and to write a comment on the bag. What a treat it is for children to have you read their parents' comments!

Put Them In Order

Reproduce the three mini-books on pages 63-68. For this activity, copy the pages on separate sheets of paper—not back-to-back. Laminate the pages, and cut them apart into separate cards. Display a four-scene story to a small group of children. Invite children to help you describe the scene and the action that is happening on each card. Use time order words to describe the sequence of the actions, such as first, second, next, and last. While children close their eyes, mix up the four cards. Ask for a volunteer to put the pictures in order. Repeat this so each child has a chance to order the pictures.

Display two sets of pictures (eight cards) in a mixed-up order. Ask, "*Which four pictures belong together?*" Let children help you order each set and tell each story.

Splash! Splash! Splash!

My Little Book of Jim

____
Name

Jim will swim.

Can you dive?

Jim will dive.

Can you swim?

Jim will jump.

Can you jump?

Do you like the snowman?

My Little Book of Nan and Jan

Name

Nan likes the snowman.

Jan likes the snow.

Nan likes the snow.

Jan likes the snowman.

Nan and Jan like the snow.

Do you like the snow?

Yum! Yum! Yum!

My Little Book of Mel and Nell

____

Name

Cut! Cut! Cut!

Nell likes melon.

Mel likes melon.

Dad cuts the melon.

Mel and Nell like melon.

Do you like melon?

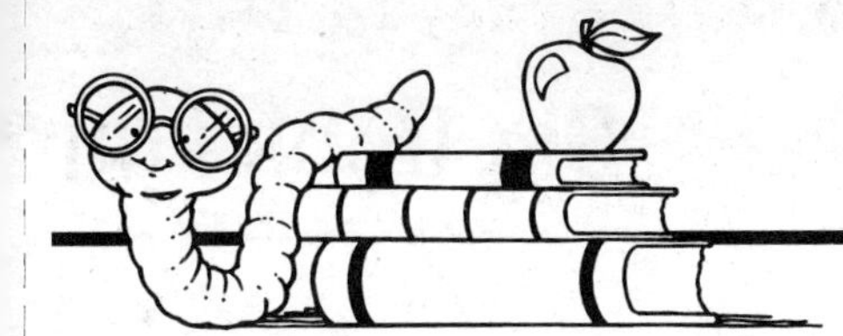

65 Living Big Books

Tear butcher paper into large pages to make a "Living Big Book." Draw a large object, such as a flower, animal, or tree, on each page so it takes up the entire space. Make sure one part of each drawing includes a round shape that can be cut out so that a child can peek through it. Let children help you decorate a cover for the book. Depending on how many book pages you have, select enough children for each page. Demonstrate how to hold a page and insert your face in the hole so you "become" part of the illustration! Have children holding the pages stand in a line in front of the rest of the group. Encourage children to make up a simple story using each illustration in sequence. After the story is finished, select different children to become part of the Living Big Book.

Turn this into a unique, imaginative event for parents on a special day. Make several of these books so each child has a page to hold. As children dictate each story, record their words exactly on each page. Parents will be snapping photos faster than you can read these Living Big Books!

66 Book Door

Transform your classroom door into a "Book Door." Collect a series of calendar pictures that show action and relate to a theme, such as kittens, puppies, or frogs. Cover your door with butcher paper. Add a decorative border. Display one of the pictures. Write a sentence on a sentence strip that describes the picture, and post the strip below the picture. The next day, change the picture and sentence. Before reading the next installment of the story, reread the first sentence to children. Do this each day until the story is finished. Children will be eager to "read" the door! As children become familiar with this activity, you might invite them to help you write a story.

67 Big Book Buddy

Make big books out of favorite songs or rhymes. Use a marker to print the words on extra-large sheets of paper. Let children help you illustrate each page. Laminate the pages for more durability and add a decorative cover made from heavy paper. Bind the pages together. Each day, select a child to be the "Big Book Buddy," who will assist you by turning the pages as you read the day's big book! Reproduce the Big Book Buddy Badges on page 71 so each child will have one to wear. Invite the Big Book Buddy to color their badge. Staple bright colors of ribbon at the bottom. Encourage the big book buddy to wear their badge while turning the pages for you!

68 Big Book Bookmarks

Reproduce the "Big Book Bookmarks" on page 72 onto sturdy paper, one bookmark for each child. Punch a hole in the bottom of each bookmark and tie on a long, colorful ribbon. Let children color their bookmarks, and tape them up in a line along the bottom of one wall. Tell children that when they want to "read" a big book, they should take their bookmarks off the wall, check out a big book, and use their bookmarks as they read. Demonstrate how to hold a bookmark horizontally under a line in a story to help track the words. When children are finished reading, remind them to return their bookmarks to the wall. This is a quick way to see how many children are at your big book center.

Big Book Buddy Badges

Big Book Bookmarks

Bite into a

BIG BOOK!

69 My Big Book

Invite children to create their own big books using nursery rhymes and favorite songs. Reproduce the "My Big Book" cover label on page 74 for each child. Invite each child to select a familiar nursery rhyme. Print the text on extra-large sheets of paper. Show children how to color their cover labels, print their names, and glue the labels onto an extra-large sheet of paper for their book covers. Give children a week's time to illustrate their books. Before binding the pages together, laminate them or cover them with clear self-stick paper for durability.

After all the big books are completed, invite children to share them with the class. Encourage young authors to hold up their books as you read the rhymes aloud. Invite parents to this special event. Display the books in a reading corner so children can read them independently or in small groups during activity time.

You can also make Big Books from commercially-printed materials if they are for your personal classroom use. Simply print the text on extra-large sheets of paper. Then use an opaque projector to enlarge the illustrations for tracing on the book pages. Invite children to help you decorate a book cover. Laminate the pages before binding them into big books.

My BIG BOOK
Name

70 Hop to It!

Choose a set of "Word Family Cards" from pages 78-82. Read them aloud to the children and then tape each card onto a carpet square. Place the squares close together on the floor in random order. Let children take turns hopping from one square to another and calling out the word taped on each square. Help any children who struggle with reading the words. This movement activity not only reinforces phonics skills, it is fun and provides an experience that encourages young children to think in a different way.

71 Word Hunt

Tape a card on each child's chest, reading the word for the child. Let children walk around the classroom searching for other words in their family. Have word families stand together. Or, place children in five groups. Assign each group a different word family and give the group one card. Hide the rest of the cards around the room. Tell groups to work together to find their rhyming word cards. Let groups stand together and take turns reading the words they found.

Word Family Books

Reproduce one set of "Word Family Cards" for each child from pages 78–82. Set up a print shop where children can create their own original word family books. Provide materials for writing, illustrating, and assembling books—white paper, stapler, construction paper, crayons, scissors, and glue.

Help each child staple ten pages together into a book. Demonstrate how to draw a book cover on the first page. Glue a word card on each of the other nine pages. Invite children to illustrate each word and decorate their book covers. Help them print their names and titles on their covers. Encourage children to read their word family books to you and to one another.

After reading aloud each book, place the student-made books in the library to share with other classes. Host a Read-to-a-Parent Day when children read aloud their books to their parents while eating a picnic lunch together. Take plenty of photographs of families reading to post on your door. Add the title "We Can Read!" You'll notice how proud both parents and children are when they see themselves in this door display.

1-57029-489-5 *101 Preschool Reading Activities*

73 Does It Belong?

Select one set of "Word Family Cards" from pages 78–82. Line them up on the chalk tray below your white board. Point to each word, encouraging children to say the words with you. While children close their eyes, insert two word cards from a different family. Challenge children to discover the words that do not belong when they open their eyes! Repeat this often so children become familiar with the words.

After children feel comfortable with this activity, ask for volunteers to insert the words that do not belong.

For a variation, line up a set of three cards from the same word family. Display three other words, one from the same word family and two from different families. Challenge children to find the correct card that matches the word family on display.

Once children learn the words, have fun placing the words one at a time on display. Begin a simple story and include each word in the story as you place it in line. Example: "Once upon a time there was a cat. The cat jumped on a fence to catch a rat. The rat leaped down on a mat. . . " Have fun with the story! Your purpose is to help children read the words.

Word Family Cards

bat	hat	rat
cat	mat	sat
fat	pat	vat

Word Family Cards

Bill	hill	pill
fill	Jill	sill
gill	mill	will

Word Family Cards

bop	lop	sop
cop	mop	top
hop	pop	stop

Word Family Cards

bell	fell	tell
cell	Nell	well
dell	sell	shell

Word Family Cards

bug	jug	rug
dug	lug	tug
hug	mug	snug

1-57029-489-5 *101 Preschool Reading Activities*

74 Books and Bracelets

Encourage children's interest in words by reading aloud the following books. This selection of books teaches a variety of phonics concepts and provides reading time fun!

Antics by Cathi Hepworth (G.P. Putnam's Sons, 1992)

The Fat Cat by Stephen Mooser (Warner Books, 1988)

Green Eggs and Ham by Dr. Seuss (Random House, 1960)

Hop on Pop by Dr. Seuss (Random House, 1963)

Make Way for Ducklings by Robert McCloskey (Viking, 1941)

Nuts to You! by Lois Ehlert (Harcourt Brace Jovanovich, 1993)

Time for Bed by Mem Fox (Harcourt Brace, 1993)

After reading aloud, help children make lists of rhyming words. Try to group the words by word families. Reproduce the "Word Family Bracelets" (page 84) on sturdy paper. Read each sentence frame aloud until children become familiar with the words. Give each child a bracelet. Invite children to dictate two rhyming words, and write them on the blanks on their bracelet. Have children color their bracelet. Help them wrap the bracelet around their wrist, taping the plain end over the TAB end. Let children take turns reading their bracelets to each other.

Word Family Bracelets

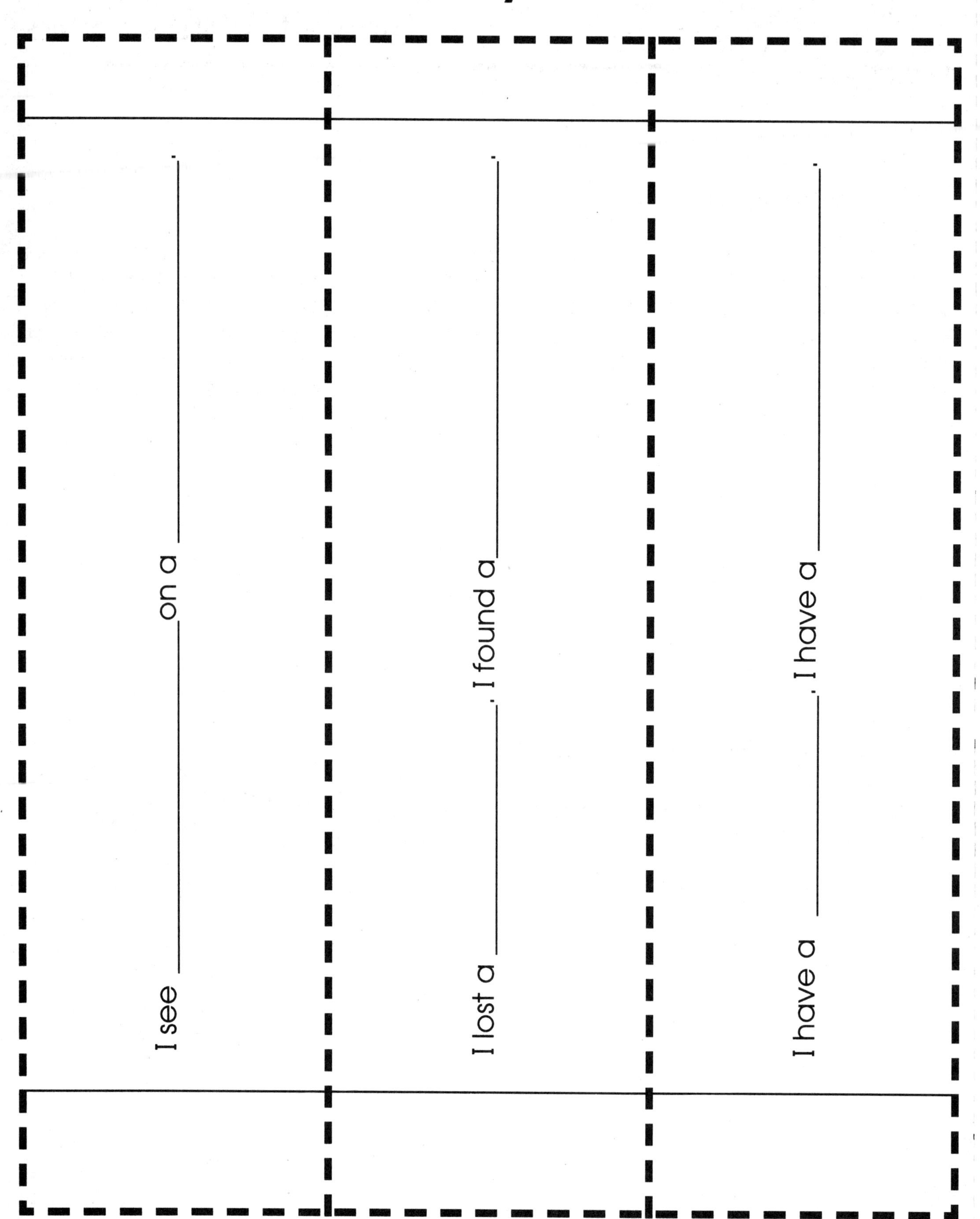

75 Picture Puzzles

Help children develop their visual discrimination and thinking skills as they arrange parts to create a whole. Reproduce the pictures on page 86 on sturdy paper. Color and laminate the pictures for more durability. Cut each picture into at least four vertical strips. Invite children to take turns arranging one set of strips to form the correct picture. After children become familiar with this activity, mix up the strips for both pictures. Challenge children to sort the strips into two groups and arrange each group to form the correct picture.

After the pictures are assembled, ask children questions such as these to stimulate thinking skills:

- What do you think is happening in this picture?
- How do you think the animals/children feel?
- How can you tell the way they feel?
- What do you think will happen next?

As a follow-up activity, give each child a 9" x 12" sheet of construction paper. Invite children to draw their own pictures. Encourage children to use the entire space for their artwork, and then laminate the drawings. Have volunteers share their drawings and tell the class what is happening in their picture. Ask children what they think might happen next in each picture. Cut each drawing in half using a simple curved, wavy, or jagged line. Place one half of each drawing in a box. Spread out the remaining halves on a table. Challenge children to take turns putting together the matching pictures. This will become a favorite activity for children as they have fun assembling their own artwork puzzles!

Picture Puzzles

Can You Remember?

Help young children develop their ability to order objects and build memory skills.

Reproduce page 88, "Can You Remember?", on sturdy paper for each child. Color the pictures, laminate them for more durability, and cut them apart. Hold three items, such as the horn, bell, and drum. Ask for a volunteer to follow your directions to order the objects. Give simple directions: Put the bell first, the horn second, and the drum last. Repeat this several times using three different objects each time. Let children take turns making up the directions. As children become more successful with ordering three items, let them try to order more than three at a time.

For a variation, ask children to close their eyes and listen carefully as you describe a simple order for three objects. Example: The whistle is first, the horn is second, and the star is last. Mix up the order of the objects. When children open their eyes, see if they can rearrange the objects correctly. This activity builds listening skills as well as develops the ability to order objects.

Can You Remember?

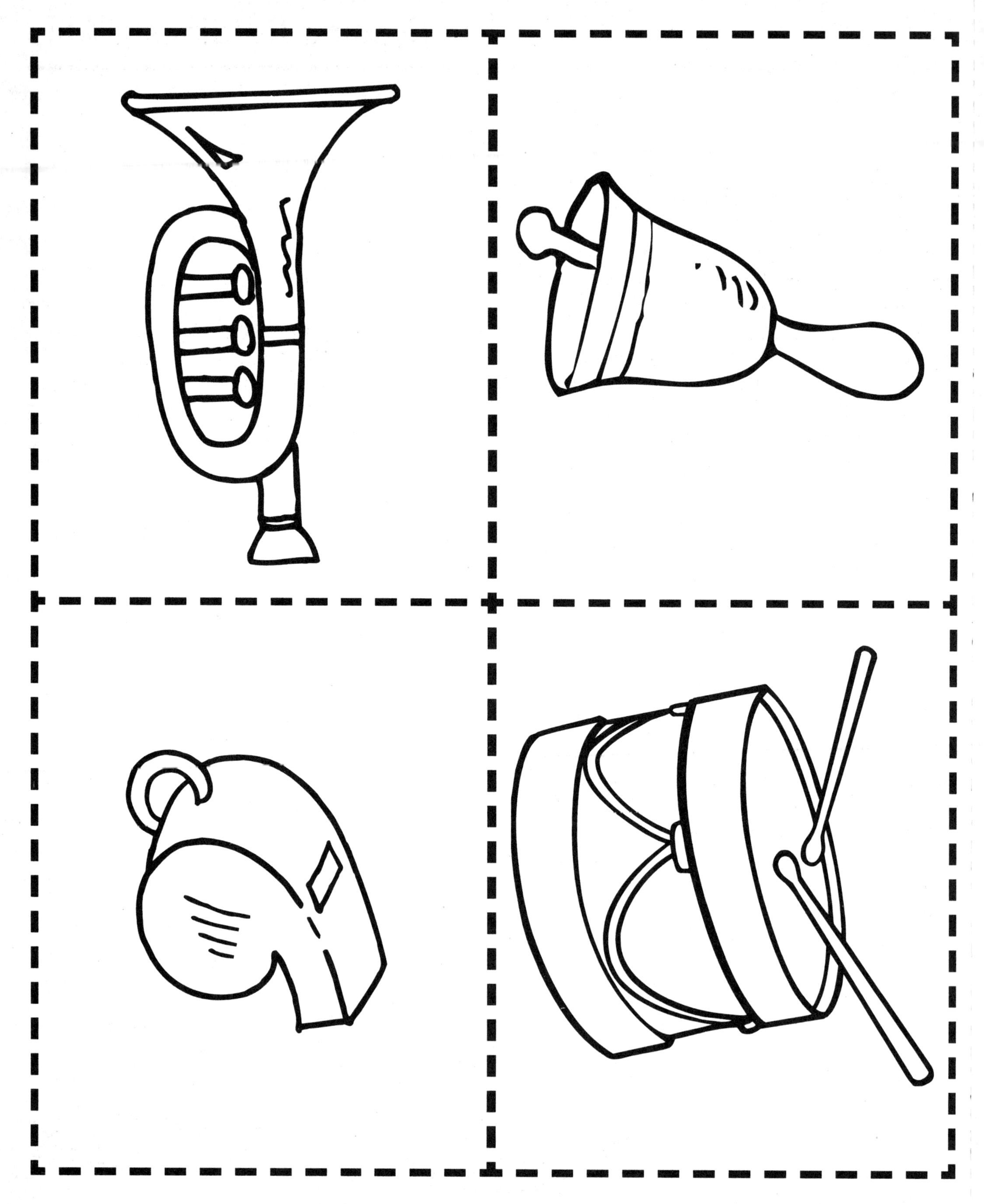

77 Sequencing Cards

Help children sequence events, practice oral language, and develop logical thinking. Reproduce both sets of "Sequencing Cards" (pages 90–91) on sturdy paper. Color and laminate the cards before cutting them apart. Display a four-step picture story, and describe each step. Tell children which picture is drawn first, second, third, and last. Mix up the order, and challenge children to tell you the correct order. Ask for volunteers to describe each step. Invite children to use the sequence of pictures to tell a story. Have each child draw a picture of what might happen next—the fifth step. Encourage all children to tell a story about their picture.

For an enrichment activity, display in order the "Fruit Bowl" sequence of steps. Set out a bowl, an apple, a banana, and grapes. Ask for volunteers to make a fruit bowl following the steps in the pictures. Let children try to draw a bowl of fruit following the step-by-step pictures. Bring in grapes and sliced apples and bananas for a delicious treat!

For another enrichment activity, display in order the "Building a House" sequence of steps. Cut out construction paper pieces that match the shape and proportion of those in the pictures—one large rectangle (house), one large triangle (roof), two small squares (windows), one small rectangle (door), one long rectangle (upper window), and one small trapezoid (chimney). Place the shapes on the floor. Let children take turns "building a house" by following the steps in the pictures. Ask a parent to help you cut out the correct shapes for a house for each child. Have children assemble their houses on construction paper and glue the pieces in place. Invite children to draw themselves and their families next to the house. Let them take turns sharing their artwork and telling a story about it.

Sequencing Cards
Fruit Bowl

Sequencing Cards
Building a House

78 Play Mats

Promote oral language and creative thinking with this fun activity! Reproduce the two play mats on pages 93–94. You might want to enlarge each mat before you copy it. Color the mats and laminate them. Tape the mats on the floor in different areas. Provide children with small manipulatives, such as buttons to represent cars and people. Invite small groups of children to move their cars along the roads, creating different routes to and from places on the mat. Encourage children to use the buttons to make up stories about families playing in the park. Let two children start their cars in the same place on the mat and find different ways to reach another place.

For enrichment, tape one of the mats on a white board. Place magnets on the board and tell children that they represent cars or people. Invite children to take turns creating a story as they move the magnetic props all around one of the mats.

For a follow-up activity, help develop children's skills in listening and following directions. Ask for volunteers to take turns moving the magnetic cars (or people) from one place to another according to the directions you give. For example, you might say this: "Place the car by the lake. Make the car move along the road to the green house. . . "

Play Town

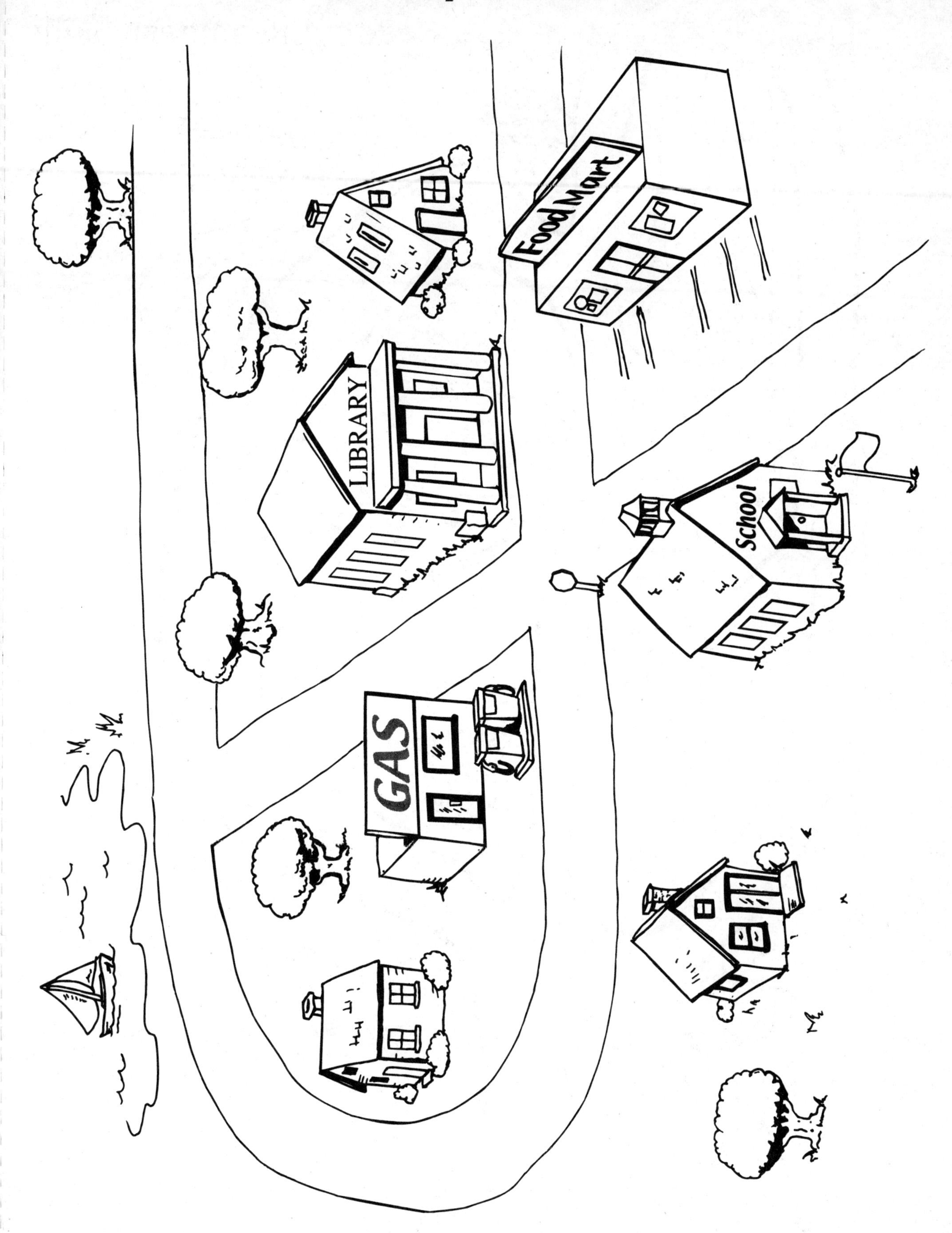

At the Park

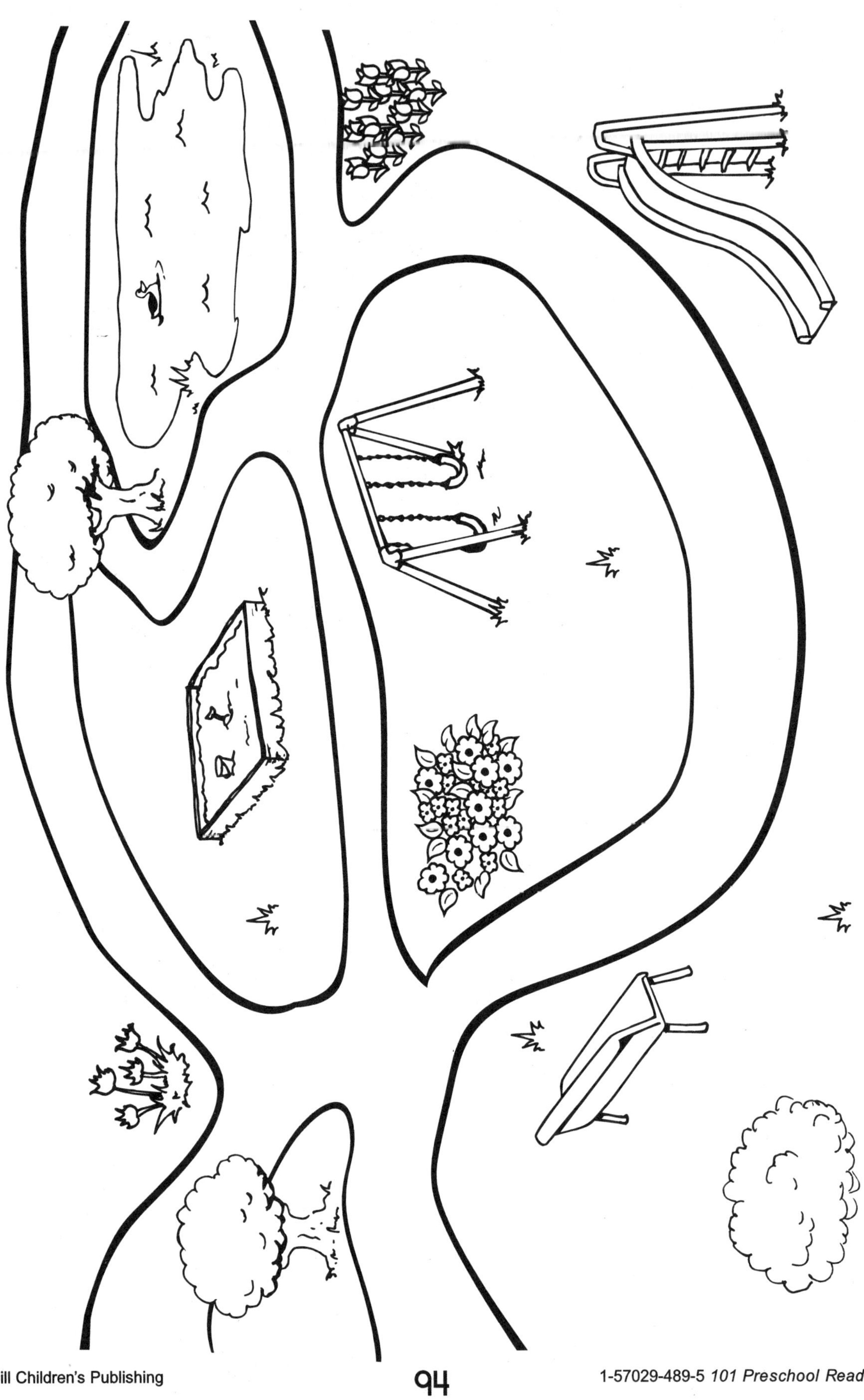

Comic Strip Fun

Develop print awareness with children and teach them that people read words moving from left to right. Laminate and cut out age-appropriate comic strips from a Sunday newspaper. Choose comics that tell a complete story with and without words. Display a comic strip. Point to each frame and read aloud the captions. Encourage children to tell what might happen next before reading the next frame. Invite children to expand the story or invent a new ending. Later, prepare a book made of pages that contain stickers and lines of arrows pointing from the left to the right. Model how to start at the sticker in the upper left corner and move a finger across the paper, following the arrows. Invite children to take turns practicing this left-right progression. Encourage each child to name the "picture stickers" and make up a story to go along with them.

Hang Up the Pairs!

Help children develop their ability to see likenesses and differences by letting them sort laundry. Put pairs of clean socks, mittens, and gloves in a basket. String a clothesline in your classroom, and set out clothespins and the basket of clothes. Invite children to take turns hanging up the laundry in matching pairs. Follow up this activity by reproducing two copies of coloring book pages that show baby animals, things that go, and other age-appropriate pictures. Mix up the pictures. Let children take turns sorting the pictures and hanging them up in pairs.

81 Nursery Rhyme Fun

What better way to give children practice in retelling a sequence of story events than by reciting nursery rhymes! Reproduce the traditional rhymes and patterns on pages 97–98, one set for each child. Teach children each nursery rhyme and move the patterns to act out the story. Invite children to read with other classmates as they manipulate their own story props.

Once children become familiar with the stories, mix up the manipulatives and invite children to help you group them into the separate rhymes, identifying each character. Encourage children to predict what happens next after the end of the story. Set out simple costumes and let children take turns dressing up as the characters and acting out the stories as the class recites the rhymes. Challenge volunteers to retell the story in their own words while children act it out in costume.

When you use "sing-song" nursery rhymes to teach prereading skills, you develop within children an appreciation for repetitive language and rhyming words.

82 Just Like Me

Help children connect events in stories to real-life experiences. Before teaching children "Jack and Jill" on page 98, discuss chores children help out with already or ones they can begin helping with at home. List these on paper. Reproduce the rhyme and story props for each child. Ask children what chore Jack and Jill had to do. Ask children what might happen after Jack and Jill fall down. Introduce unfamiliar vocabulary such as crown. Challenge children to use crown or other new term, in their spoken language throughout the day.

Nursery Rhyme Fun

"Jack Be Nimble"

Jack be nimble,
Jack be quick,
Jack jump over
The candlestick.

"Hey, Diddle Diddle"

Hey, diddle diddle,
The cat and the fiddle,
The cow jumped over the moon.
The little dog laughed
To see such sport,
And the dish ran away
With the spoon!

Nursery Rhyme Fun

"Jack and Jill"

Jack and Jill went up the hill
To fetch a pail of water.
Jack fell down,
And broke his crown,
And Jill came tumbling after.

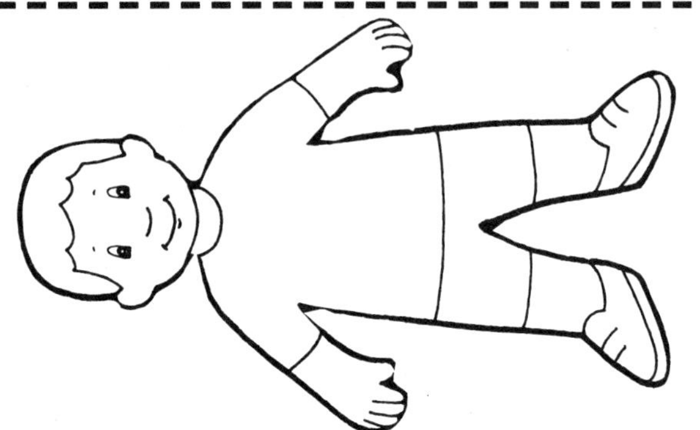

"Hickory, Dickory, Dock"

Hickory, dickory, dock,
The mouse ran up the clock.
The clock struck one.
The mouse ran down.
Hickory, dickory, dock.

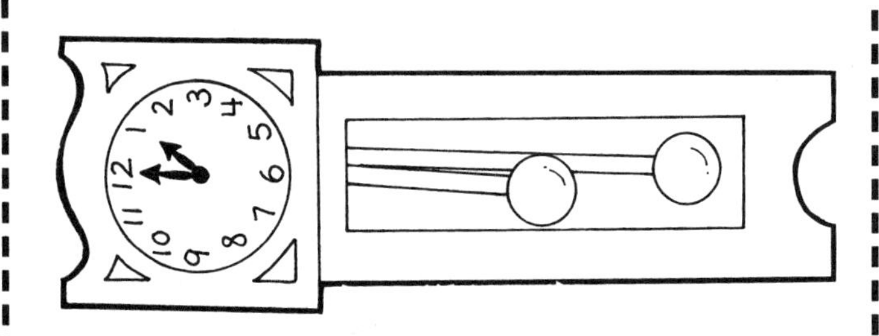

1-57029-489-5 *101 Preschool Reading Activities*

Textured Letters

Learning to connect the names of letters with their shapes is an essential part of learning to read and to write. Cut out two small tagboard cards for each letter of the alphabet. Using a glue bottle, draw the letters of the alphabet one at a time on separate cards. Each letter will have two cards—one uppercase, the other lowercase. You may want to sketch a line to show how the lowercase letters "sit" on a line. This will help children distinguish between b, d, p, g, q, n, and u. Sprinkle sand or rice over the glue. Let dry. Place three to five sequential pairs of letters in a paper sack. Invite children to take turns emptying the bag and matching the letter pairs. Encourage children to trace over each textured letter with their fingers. Repeat this with other sets until children practice matching all the letters. As a follow-up activity, place each set of letters in a paper sack. Let children take turns pulling out a letter and identifying it. Once children become familiar with the letters and their shapes, sit them in a circle. While children close their eyes, give each child a textured letter card. Ask children to try and identify their letters just by touch.

Extend this same idea by making textured puzzle cards for the letters. Make each puzzle by using a glue bottle to print an uppercase letter on the left-hand side of a card and the matching lowercase letter on the right-hand side. Sprinkle sand or rice over the glue. Let dry. Next, cut each card into interlocking puzzle pieces. Set out several puzzles at a time. Invite children to take turns putting the puzzles together.

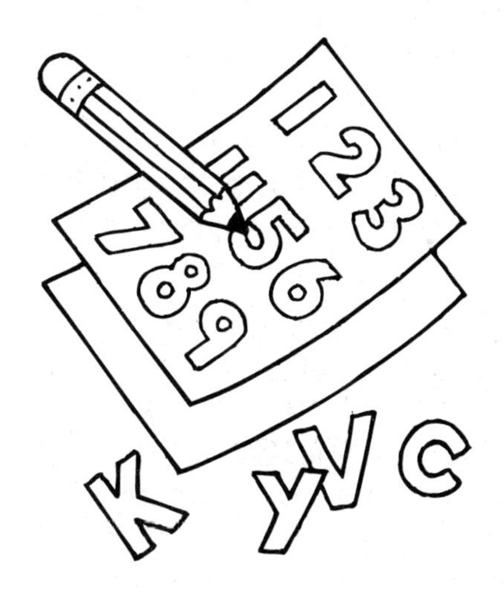

84 ABC Movement Fun

Prepare young children for reading by giving them active practice in identifying the printed alphabet.

Use chalk to print letters of the alphabet in order within a hopscotch grid. Invite children to take turns hopping from one square to the next, naming each letter on a square. Continue with other letters.

Play "Red, Rover, Red, Rover." Print the letters of the alphabet on separate large cards so they can easily be seen at a distance. Punch a hole in the top of each card and tie on a length of yarn. Give each child a card to wear. Go outside and place children in two groups. Have groups hold hands and stand side by side about 15 feet away from each other. Choose one group to start. Help the group decide which letter from the other team it wants to call over. Lead the group in calling, "Red, Rover, Red, Rover, let *alphabet letter* come over!" Encourage the child wearing that letter to run between two children on the opposite team and break their hand clasp. If the runner does this, tell the child to choose someone from the group to join the runner's group. If the hand clasp holds, invite the runner to join the new group! Play until all letters are called.

As a follow-up, have children sit in a circle. Give each child a letter card to wear. Let children take turns standing up and performing actions that begin with the letters they are wearing. For example, a child wearing C could clap hands and a child wearing Z could zoom around the circle.

85 ABC's To Go

Reproduce on cardstock the "Alphabet Squares" on page 103 onto tagboard for each child. Cut out the cards and place each set in a self-sealing plastic bag. Label each bag with a child's name. Print simple high-frequency words such as *the, a, an, and, he,* and *she* on separate cards. Invite each child to choose a word card, and then pull out letter squares from his or her bag to "spell" the word.

To enhance the on-the-move aspect of this traveling alphabet, include a note in the zip-lock bags along with the alphabet squares. Instruct parent and child to label items at home with the appropriate letters in the bag. Families can draw an alphabet map of items in their home and return it to school for children to share. This is truly an alphabet adventure!

86 Alphabet Puppets

Reproduce "Alphabet Squares" on page 103. Laminate the page and cut apart the squares. Glue each square on one end of a craft stick to make a puppet. Sit children in a circle, giving each child one or two puppets. Tell children that when you make the sound of their letter, they should hold up their puppet. For example: Call out "buh, buh, buh", and prompt children to look for the letter b puppet.

Read an alphabet book from this list or one of your favorites. Have children hold up the appropriate puppet when each letter is read.

Alphabatics by Suse MacDonald (Bradbury Press, 1986)

Alphabet Times Four: An International ABC by Ruth Brown (Dutton, 1991)

From Acorn to Zoo and Everything in Between in Alphabetical Order by Satoshi Kitamura (Sunburst, 1995)

Potluck by Anne Shelby (Orchard, 1991)

Tomorrow's Alphabet by George Shannon (Mulberry Books, 1999)

Alphabet Squares

a	b	c	d
e	f	g	h
i	j	k	l
m	n	o	p
q	r	s	t
u	v	w	x
	y	z	

Alphabet Scrapbook and Train

Help children begin to recognize beginning letters in familiar words. First, make an Alphabet Scrapbook by putting together 26 large sheets of white construction paper. Punch holes on the left-hand side and insert metal rings to create a book. Label the pages A through Z. Each day, highlight one letter. Cut out large examples of the letter from titles in magazines and newspapers. Cut out calendar and magazine pictures showing names that begin with that letter. Invite children to glue the pictures and cutout letters on the page. Do this for each letter. Next, cut out large examples of high-frequency words. Place them in a basket near the scrapbook. Encourage children to glue the words on the appropriate pages. Place the finished book in a reading area for children to enjoy.

Follow up by reproducing the "Alphabet Train" on page 105 for each child. Have children trace each letter to help develop their fine motor coordination. Invite them to put the train pieces in alphabetical order. Give children an envelope to store their trains so they can practice ordering the alphabet at another time or at home.

Duck Pond

With practice, young children can successfully start to identify rhyming sounds in familiar words. Make a copy of the "Duck Pond" on page 106. Choose a word family, and print its rime (the part of the single syllable word from the vowel onward) on the pond. Print a word that belongs to the word family on four of the ducks and two words that do not belong on the remaining ducks. Reproduce this sheet for each child. Review the word family with children. Let them cut out the ducklings and glue the appropriate ones on the pond. Repeat this for different word families.

Alphabet Train

Duck Pond

89 What Starts With A?

Reproduce the "Alphabet Strip" on page 108, one for each child. Help children cut out the strips and tape them together to make the alphabet. Tell children to lay their strips in front of them. Have children color the individual letter tiles—the top row yellow (a–g), the second row red (h–n), the third row green (o–u), and the bottom row blue (v–z). Help them cut out the letter tiles and store the tiles in a self-sealing plastic bag. Teach children "The Alphabet Song." As they sing, have them point to each letter on their strips. Have them spread out their letter tiles. To help children hear the sounds the letters can make, say each child's name and have children find that letter tile. Ask what other words begin with that letter.

Example: Alyssa, your name begins with an A. (Make the short a sound.) Let's find the yellow letter tile for A. What other words begin with the same sound? (Antonio, ant . . .) Finally, reproduce *All About Me* on page 109 for each child. Invite children to draw a self-portrait. Help them write the letter their name begins with and then their name. These make treasured displays for the refrigerator!

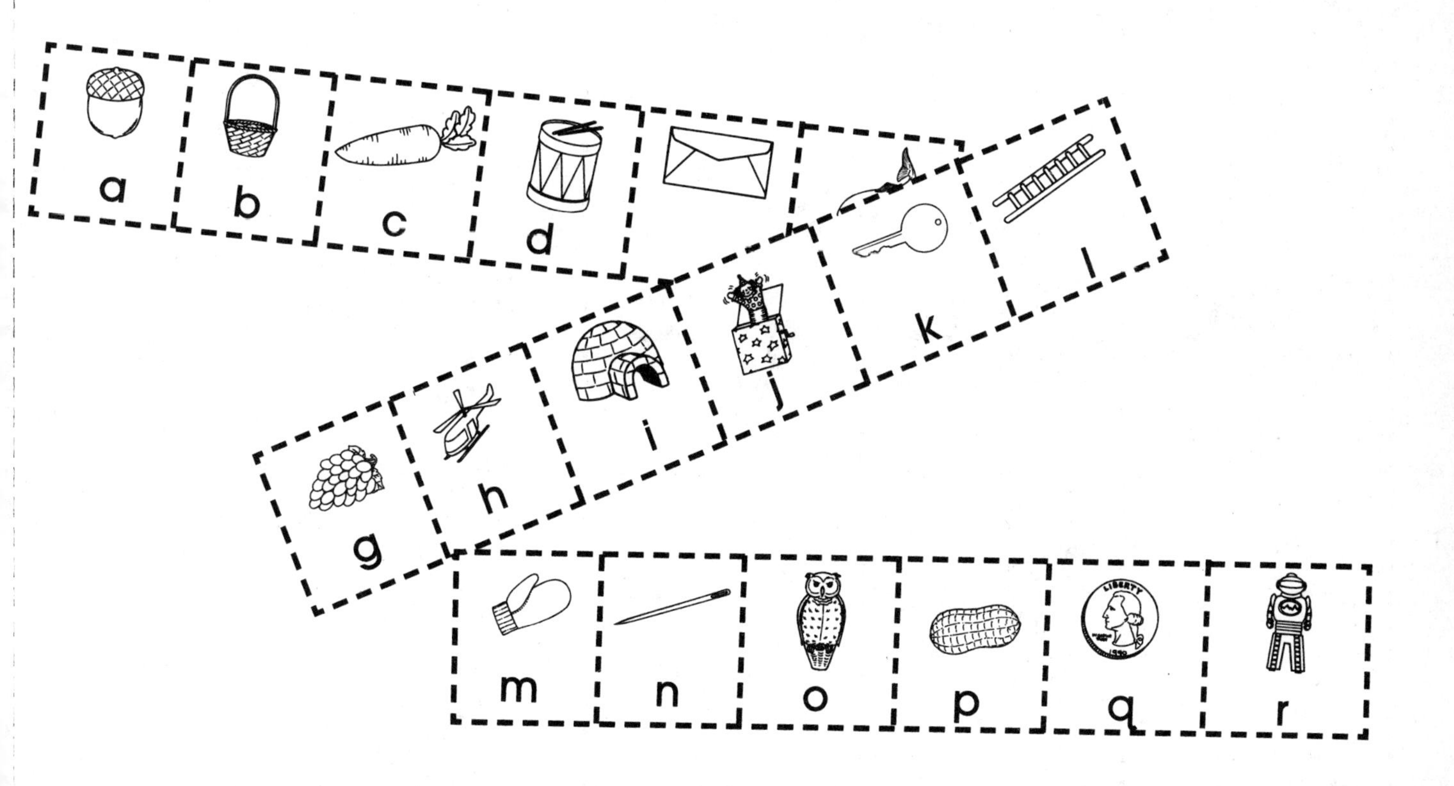

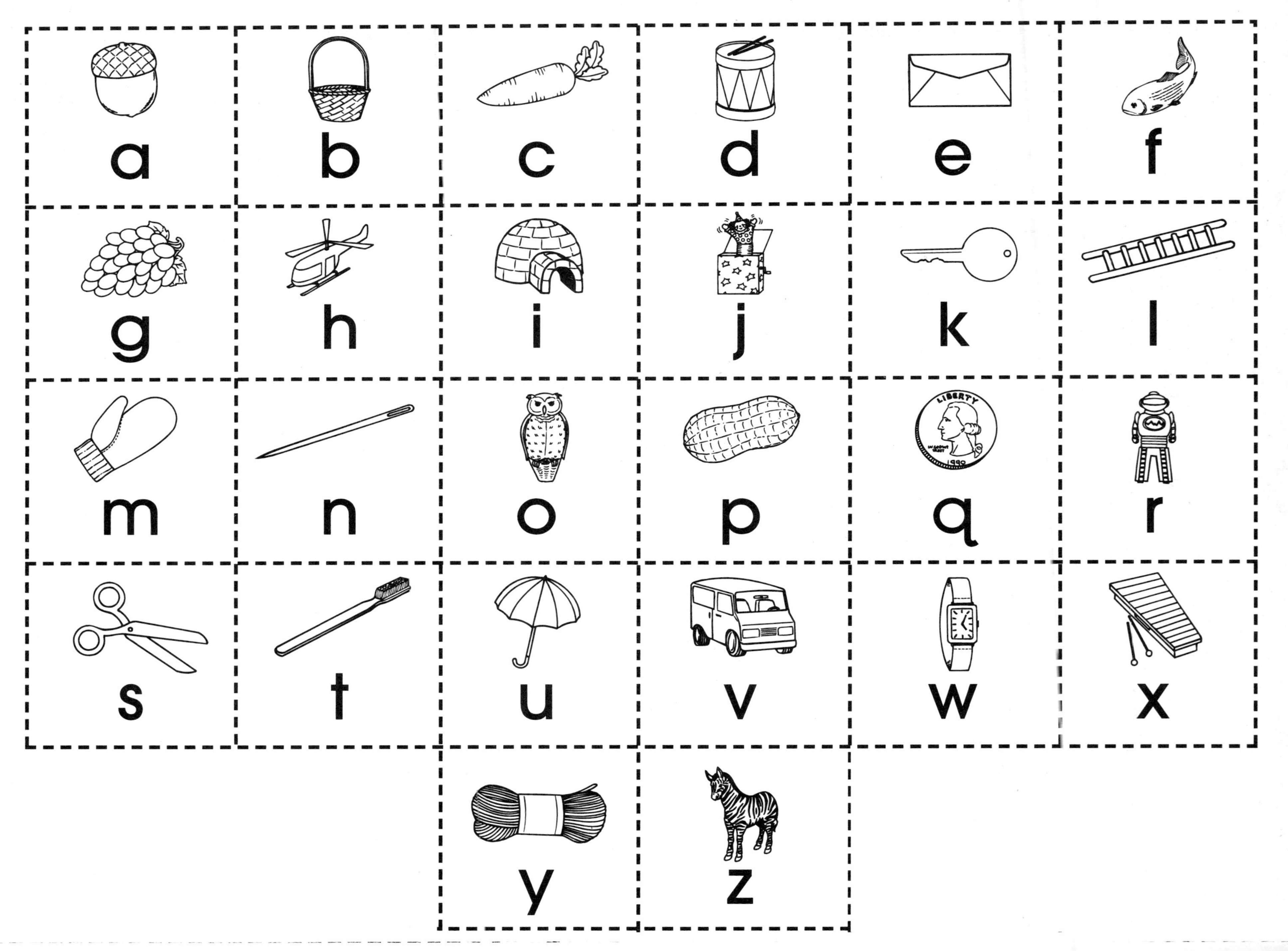
a
b
c
d
e
f
g
h
i
j
k
l
m
n
o
p
q
r
s
t
u
v
w
x
y
z

All About Me

90 A Story Web

Reading a wide array of books helps children understand an increasingly difficult and varied vocabulary. After reading a book, invite children to sit in a circle. Hold a ball of yarn and begin with a sentence to retell the story. Then, while holding onto the end of the yarn, roll the ball to a child, who will tell the next part of story. Repeat this until the story is finished and a story web of yarn is woven!

Here are some books for your "read-aloud" library:

Big Fat Hen illustrated by Keith Baker (Harcourt Brace, 1994): One very big hen counts to ten with her feathered friends and their chicks.

Bringing the Rain to Kapiti Plain by Verna Aardema (Dutton, 1993): The text is written in verse and tells the story of how a herder named Ki-pat makes it rain.

Brown Bear, Brown Bear, What Do You See? by Bill Martin, Jr. (Holt, 1996): One colorful animal after another sees the next animal until the surprising ending!

Chicka Chicka Boom Boom by Bill Martin, Jr. and John Archambault (Simon and Schuster, 1989): An imaginative rhyming tale about letters of the alphabet climbing up and tumbling down from a coconut tree in the tropics!

Moving Day by Robert Kalan (Greenwillow Books, 1996): A hermit crab searching underwater for a new home tries out many different seashells before finding the right one.

Suddenly! by Colin McNaughton (Harcourt Brace, 1995): Preston Pig outsmarts a hungry wolf trying to catch him!

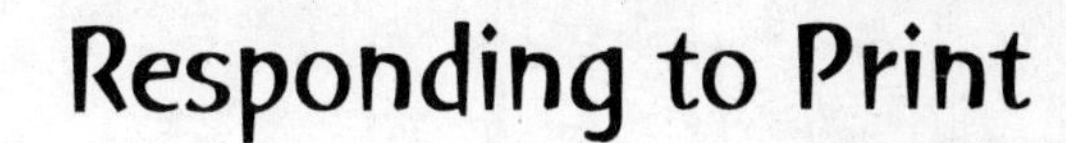

91 Magazine Corner

Introducing children to appropriate magazines exposes them to a variety of different types of print—poems, riddles, stories, games, puzzles, posters, and more. Set up a Magazine Corner in your classroom. Place magazines in a basket. Provide children with small poster paper, crayons, pencils, stickers, scissors, and other creative writing tools. Encourage children to respond to what they "read" by drawing mini-posters about their favorite parts in the magazines. Let children dictate a sentence about their poster, and record their exact words below the artwork. This experience will help children understand that writing is used to communicate ideas and information.

Here are some excellent children's magazines and contact addresses. You may also want to look at their Web sites.

Babybug
P.O. Box 9304
LaSalle, IL 61301-9897
This board-book style magazine contains colorful illustrations of stories and rhymes. Ladybug, by the same publisher, is for older preschoolers.
(Ages 6 months to 2 years)

Sesame Street Magazine
Children's Television Workshop
One Lincoln Plaza
New York, NY 10023
This delightful magazine features Sesame Street characters who illustrate rhymes, stories, posters, puzzles, and more.
(Ages 2–6 years)

Your Big Backyard
National Wildlife Federation
8925 Leesburg Pike
Vienna, VA 22184
Delightful drawings and nature photographs illustrate stories, informational articles, poems, games, and riddles written in simple text.
(Ages 3–6 years)

92 Funny Faces

Develop children's listening skills and ability to make predictions with this activity. Reproduce "Funny Faces" (page 113) on tagboard. Color or paint the smiley face red, and laminate it for more durability. Tape the face to a ruler or paint stick to make a "stop sign." As you read a story, pause at various parts, hold up the stop sign, and ask children to guess what will probably happen next. Children will want to be successful in guessing where the story is going, so accept all responses. Children will automatically be ready to respond when they see your stop sign.

Extend this activity by reproducing "Funny Faces" (page 113) on tagboard for each child. Invite children to color and cut out both faces. Help each child put two faces back to back, and then tape or glue a large craft stick between the faces. (Paint sticks and rulers also work.) At story time, tell children that you will be asking questions while you read. Explain that you want them to respond by showing you their happy face or sad face. Begin by sharing the title of the story. Ask, "Do you think this will be a happy or sad tale?" As you read, pause and ask questions to let children express their feelings about what is happening or what the characters are doing. Examples: "Do you think the gingerbread boy felt good about running away?" Do you think the old woman felt sad?" Whether all children respond or not, their interest will be piqued, and they'll listen much more carefully.

Funny Faces

93 Wordless Books

Sharing wordless picture books with children will develop children's creative thinking skills and invite them to use their imaginations. Below is a list of books without words. As you advance through a book, ask children what they think the story is about. Tell the story together; let children take turns describing what is happening in each illustration. Ask for volunteers to identify people, animals, or objects on each page. Let children check out the books to take home and "read" to their families. This is a great way to motivate children to learn to read!

As a follow-up activity, cut out simple pictures of animals, objects, and people. Staple together five sheets of paper to make a book for each child. Invite children to create their own wordless book by gluing one picture on each page. Encourage children to read their books to the class.

A Boy, a Dog, and a Frog by Mercer Mayer (Econo-Clad Books, 1999): A boy and a dog attempt to capture a frog.

Do You Want to Be My Friend? by Eric Carle (HarperCollins, 1995): A tiny mouse keeps asking his animal friends, "Do you want to be my friend?"

Pancakes for Breakfast by Tomie dePaola (Voyager Books, 1990): As she tries to make breakfast pancakes, a sweet elderly lady struggles because of her lack of ingredients and the help she gets from her pets.

Tuesday by David Wiesner (Clarion, 1991): A town is deluged with extraterrestrial frogs flying on lily pads!

94 Ant and Grasshopper

Help children connect events in books with real-life experiences and feelings as they create endings to open-ended tales. Reproduce "Ant and Grasshopper", (a simplified version of this Aesop's fable) on pages 116–117 for each child. The mini-book is designed to be photocopied on both sides of one sheet of paper. Invite children to color the pictures, and then help them assemble the pages into a book. (Cut along the dotted line, fold on the solid lines, arrange the pages in order, and staple them near the spine.) Read the fable together. Talk about chores that children help with at home and in the classroom. Discuss the differences between work and play. Ask questions such as these: "Would you share your food with Grasshopper if you were Ant? Have you ever asked to share something that a friend or family member had? What do you think Ant was thinking when Grasshopper asked him to share his food?"

Let children take turns creating an ending for the tale. Give children a sheet of paper to illustrate what they think happened. Encourage children to dictate their endings to you, and record the endings near their artwork. Invite volunteers to share their pictures and story endings. This is a meaningful activity to help children begin to understand that there are many different possibilities for the ending of stories, as well as for the beginning and middle.

Grasshopper played in the sun.

"I promise to work."

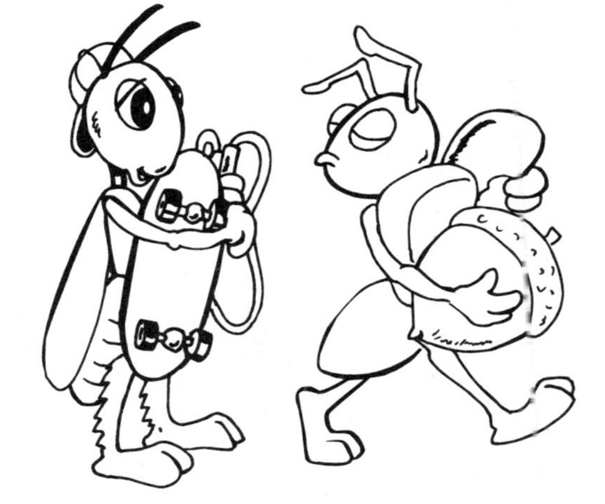

"No, Grasshopper. You played."

"Please, Ant."
Ant worked
in the sun.
"Please Share."
Snow fell.

95 Print Shop

Help children grow in understanding the different purposes of forms of print—letters, signs, lists, messages, and menus. Set up a Print Shop in your classroom. Set out menus, postcards, and other types of print mediums as well as paper, pens, markers, and pencils. Include a typewriter if you have one. Invite children to work at the Print Shop to create signs for the classroom, menus for snack time, letters and messages for friends, or other information. Insert a sheet of typing paper and demonstrate how to type a few alphabet. Set out a telephone and role-play how to answer the phone and take messages. Encourage children to write messages and letters, put them inside of envelopes, and deliver them to their friends.

If you have a computer in your classroom, let each child dictate a story to you as you input the child's exact words on the keyboard. Invite children to sit next to you as you key in their words so they can watch the letters and words form on the monitor. This will help children connect the sounds in words with their letter forms. When a child's story is finished, print out a copy and let the child illustrate it. Invite children to share their artwork as you read aloud their stories. Bind these in a class book for children to read again and again.

96 Word Walk

To build children's awareness of print in the community, take them on a Word Walk around the local neighborhood. If possible, make this a field trip to a local restaurant for lunch! Let children help you design an invitation for the field trip, and have them take it home for their parents to read. Inform parent field trip volunteers ahead of time about your purpose—to help children recognize print in street signs, billboards, shop advertisements, and menus. Encourage parents to point these out to children on the way to the restaurant and when inside the building.

After returning to the classroom, invite children to write a story about their Word Walk. Assemble large sheets of poster paper together into a book form. Let children help you title the book, illustrate it, and write the words. By following print as it is read aloud, children will begin to recognize the association between the spoken and written words.

Extend this activity by having children help make a giant thank-you card. Print "Thank you!" on the front of a sheet of poster paper. Let children help decorate the card with letters and designs as well as sign their names.

97 Parts of a Book

Model for children how to handle books carefully as they take books from the shelves and return them. Demonstrate how to hold a book and turn the pages as you read. Model how to gently open a book and smooth out its pages. Point out the front and back covers and spine of a book. Help children identify its title, author, and illustrator. Display several books. Invite volunteers to take turns pointing out the front, back, title, author, and illustrator of each book. Discuss how titles help readers know what the books are about. Explain that authors write the books and illustrators draw the pictures.

When you read a book, begin by asking different children to point to the title, the author, and the other parts of the book. Start the story by saying, "This is the beginning of the story." Do the same for the middle and end of the story. By moving your finger across the page as you read, you will help children recognize how printed letters and words flow. As you turn the pages slowly, help children understand that reading involves viewing one page at a time in order from front to back. Encourage children to be "Reader of the Day" by reading a wordless picture book to the class. (See page 114 for a book list.) Encourage the reader to point out the different parts of the book as well as review how to handle a book.

On the Road to Reading!

Provide opportunities for children to become authors by letting them create their own wordless books. Prepare a blank book for each child by stapling together sheets of white paper. Reproduce the "Front Cover" on page 122 for each child. Staple a front cover and a back cover tp each book. Cut out pictures from old calendars, magazines, and greeting cards. Invite children to select and glue a picture on each page of their books. Help them write titles and names on their front covers. Let children take turns "reading" their books to the class.

For a follow-up activity, draw the outline of a large school bus on mural paper. Draw one large window on the bus for every two children. Make sure you draw yourself as the driver! Let children color the bus yellow and draw self-portraits of themselves in the windows. Title the mural "On the Road to Reading." Ask other teachers if your authors could visit their classrooms and read their books. Pin up the mural in each room as a backdrop for your young authors.

Reading Aloud

Help children develop an interest in listening to and responding to a variety of literature—fiction, nonfiction, and poetry. Look for books that offer a diversity of settings—an inner city, a rural area, a town. Select books that feature diversity in family situations and plots, including characters with disabilities. Young children need to hear stories that have familiar settings to make them feel secure, yet they need to learn about unfamiliar places, characters, and situations to help them grow in understanding about the world around them. Read and reread the children's favorite books so they become familiar with the language of books and story forms. You are also helping children recognize books by their covers, and soon they will be picking out which books they want you to read! Choose books with repetitive language patterns to build an appreciation for rhyme and rhythm. Invite children to chant along with you once they become familiar with the language. Make sure you ask children if they have any questions about a story and if they like it and why. Help children link what they learn from a story with what they already know. Choose books that you personally enjoy reading. Your enthusiasm is contagious and will quickly build a love of reading in children!

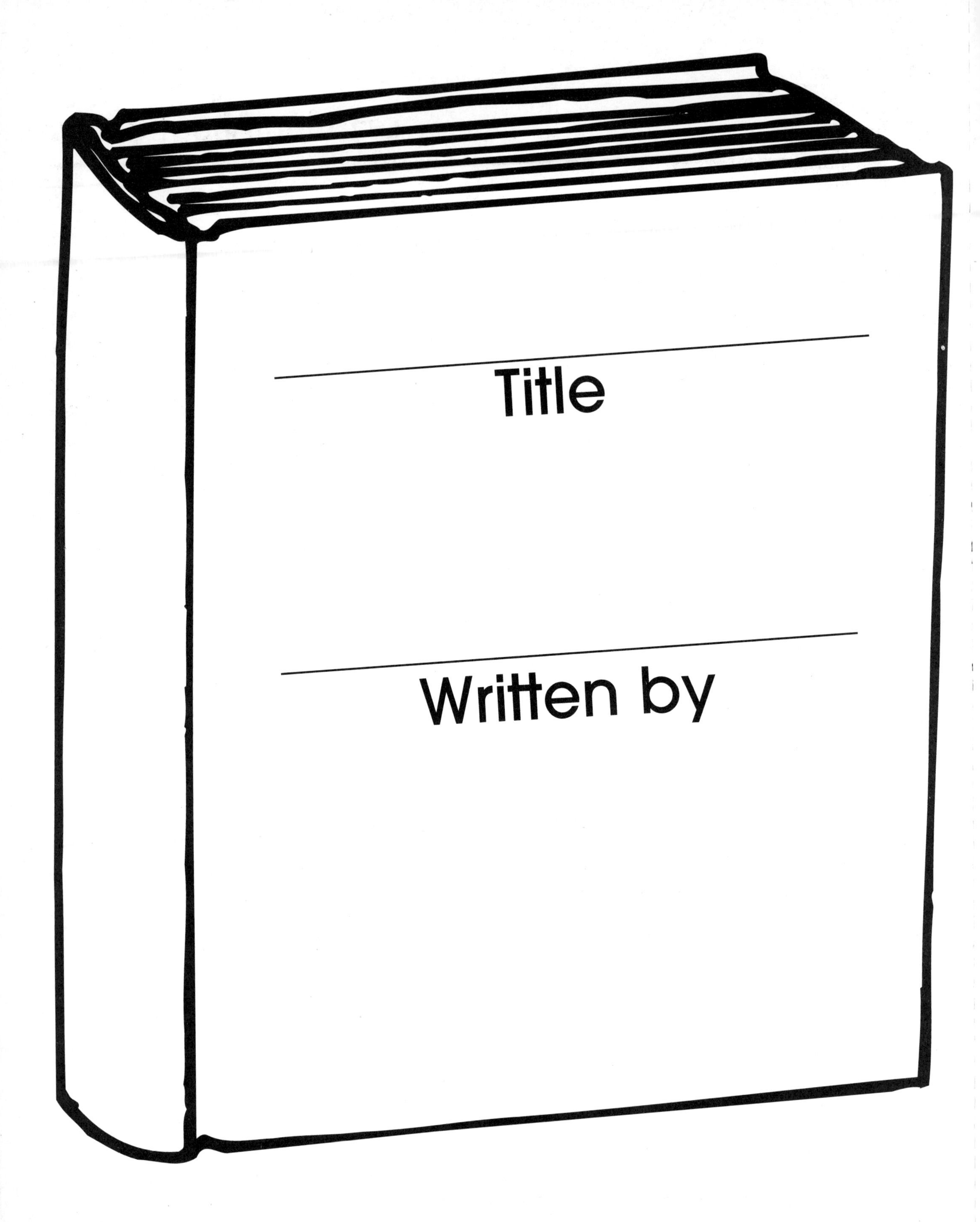
Title
Written by

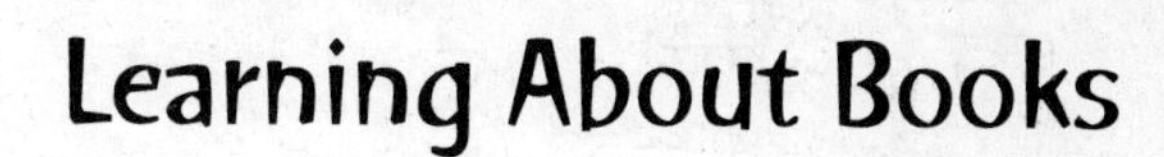

Be a Librarian!

Invite children to pretend to be librarians. Let them take turns modeling how to hold a book and turn the pages to read the story. Ask for volunteers one at a time to choose a book, and then point out features of the book, such as the front cover, the author, the illustrator, and the title. Encourage each librarian to read a book to the class. After a librarian has demonstrated her book knowledge, present the librarian with one of the book awards on pages 125 and 126. Reproduce the awards on sturdy paper. Print each child's name on an award, and then laminate the awards. They will become long-lasting treasures in each family's home!

101 Off to the Library!

Take children on a field trip to a local library. Talk with the children's librarian ahead of time and schedule your trip for a one-time special story time session. Reproduce the bookmarks on page 127 for this event. Plan ahead to let each child choose a bookmark, color it, and write his name on it. Then laminate the bookmarks and use them as nametags for your field trip.

After the trip, let children make up stories about their experiences. Bind these stories into a class book. Let children take turns reading their stories to the class. Some children may even want to dramatize their stories! Invite children to take their bookmarks home to use when reading their own books with their families. Distribute copies of the "Family Readers Award" on page 128, and have children take them home as well.

is BIG on BOOKS!

Congratulations!

Date

Your Teacher

I can read!

Great Job, ______________________

Date ______________ ______________ Your Teacher

Bookmarks

Reading Rocks

Books

are

COOL

I can

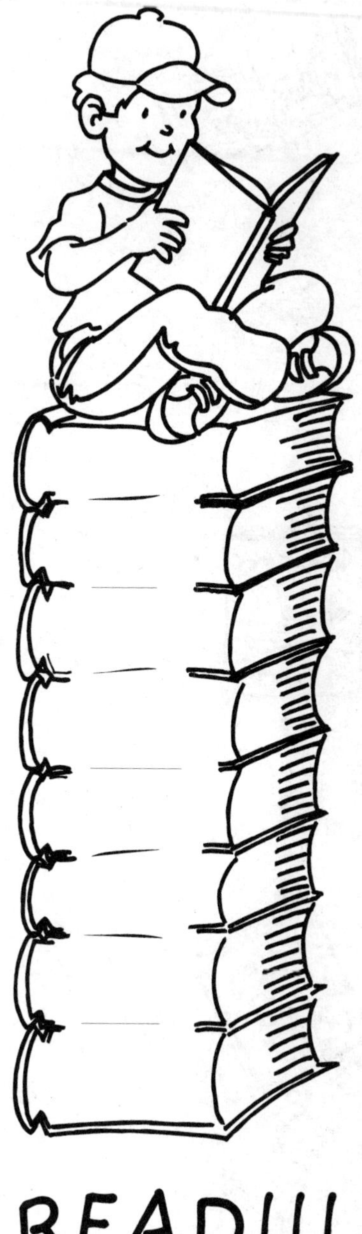

READ!!!

We are a family
of readers!
name of child and family
The Sunny Day
Poems
PUBLIC LIBRARY
ALL ABOUT EGYPT
LEARN ABOUT EGYPT
MYSTERIES
Adventures at Sea
Puzzlers
PUBLIC LIBRARY
PUBLIC LIBRARY